MY SOUL
Thirsts
for GOD

MY SOUL

Thirsts for GOD

DISCOVERY HOUSE

PUBLISHERS®

Feeding the Soul with the Word of God

©2009 by Discovery House Publishers
All rights reserved.

Our Daily Bread® is a registered trademark of RBC Ministries, Grand Rapids, MI.

Discovery House Publishers is affiliated with RBC Ministries, Grand Rapids, Michigan.

Discovery House books are distributed to the trade exclusively by Barbour Publishing, Inc., Uhrichsville, Ohio.

Library of Congress Cataloging-in-Publication Data

My soul thirsts for God : reflections on the Psalms from Our daily bread.
    p. cm.
  ISBN 978-1-57293-324-8
  1. Bible. O.T. Psalms--Meditations. I. Discovery House Publishers. II. Bible. O.T. Psalms.
English. New International. Selections. 2009. III. Our daily bread.
  BS1430.54.M9 2009
  242'.5--dc22   2009012274

Requests for permission to quote from this book should be directed to: Permissions Department, Discovery House Publishers, P.O. Box 3566, Grand Rapids, Michigan 49501.

Interior design by Matthew Van Zomeren

Printed in the United States of America
09 10 11 12 13 /BPI/ 10 9 8 7 6 5 4 3 2

Contents

Foreword

It's called "the songbook of Scripture" and "the most read book of the Bible." From the opening verse of Psalm 1, "Blessed is the man" to the closing exclamation of Psalm 150, "Let everything that has breath praise the Lord!" readers throughout the ages have found comfort, encouragement, and hope for every circumstance of life.

Now, in this one volume, we have compiled this selection of 92 daily meditations focused on the most beloved book of the Bible drawn from the world's most beloved daily devotional, *Our Daily Bread*.

You will enjoy the rich teaching and writings of twenty-one favorite *ODB* writers, such as David Roper, Joanie Yoder, Henry Bosch, David McCasland, Julie Ackerman Link, Dave Branon, Richard and Mart DeHaan.

The Publisher

Psalm 1

[1] Blessed is the man
   who does not walk in the counsel of the wicked
or stand in the way of sinners
   or sit in the seat of mockers.
[2] But his delight is in the law of the LORD,
   and on his law he meditates day and night.
[3] He is like a tree planted by streams of water,
   which yields its fruit in season
and whose leaf does not wither.
   Whatever he does prospers.

[4] Not so the wicked!
   They are like chaff
   that the wind blows away.
[5] Therefore the wicked will not stand in the judgment,
   nor sinners in the assembly of the righteous.

[6] For the LORD watches over the way of the righteous,
   but the way of the wicked will perish.

Let's Get Growing

Several years ago my interest in flowers had our home resembling a nursery. There's something about the presence of growing plants that I find very enjoyable. As I daily inspected their progress, I gained from my little green friends a new appreciation of the joy and necessity of the wonderful process of growth.

As Christians, we too are like plants. We should put down our roots, break up through the earth, spread out our branches, and burst into blossom. Such a thriving condition, however, isn't always evident in our lives. It's so easy to become bored and listless in the bland routine of our daily activities. Often we just hang on and merely exist without moving steadily toward maturity and fruitfulness.

At such times we are at a spiritual standstill and must allow Jesus the "sun of righteousness" (Malachi 4:2) to warm our hearts anew with His love. We must send our roots deep into the Word of God by meditating on it day and night (Psalm 1:2). Then we will be like a fruitful tree planted by rivers of living water, and our branches will extend outward in an ever-increasing influence and witness. They will be filled with blossoms that reflect the beauty of righteous living.

If we've become dormant, let's get growing!

—*Mart DeHaan*

Psalm 2

¹Why do the nations conspire
    and the peoples plot in vain?
²The kings of the earth take their stand
    and the rulers gather together
 against the LORD
    and against his Anointed One.
³"Let us break their chains," they say,
    "and throw off their fetters."

⁴The One enthroned in heaven laughs;
    the Lord scoffs at them.
⁵Then he rebukes them in his anger
    and terrifies them in his wrath, saying,
⁶"I have installed my King
    on Zion, my holy hill."

⁷I will proclaim the decree of the LORD:
    He said to me, "You are my Son;
    today I have become your Father.
⁸Ask of me,
    and I will make the nations your inheritance,
    the ends of the earth your possession.
⁹You will rule them with an iron scepter;
    you will dash them to pieces like pottery."

10   Therefore, you kings, be wise;
    be warned, you rulers of the earth.
11   Serve the LORD with fear
    and rejoice with trembling.
12   Kiss the Son, lest he be angry
    and you be destroyed in your way,
 for his wrath can flare up in a moment.
    Blessed are all who take refuge in him.

What Makes God Laugh?

I was washing my car one evening as the sun was preparing to kiss the earth goodnight. Glancing up, I impulsively pointed the hose at it as if to extinguish its flames. The absurdity of my action hit me, and I laughed.

Then I thought of God's laughter in Psalm 2. Wicked nations were plotting to overthrow God's anointed, thus ultimately opposing the Almighty himself. But He sits in the heavens, calm and unthreatened. Man's boldest efforts to oppose such awesome power are ludicrous. The Almighty doesn't even rise from His throne; He just laughs in derision.

But is this a heartless or cruel laughter? No! His same infinite greatness that mocks man's defiance also marks His sympathy for man in his lost condition. He's the same God who takes no pleasure in the death of the wicked (Ezekiel 33:11). And He was the incarnate Savior who wept over Jerusalem when His own people rejected Him (Matthew 23:37–39). He is great in judgment but also in compassion (Exodus 34:6–7).

God's laughter gives us the assurance that Christ will ultimately triumph over evil. Any defiance of Him and His will is futile. Instead of opposing the Son, we should submit to the Lord Jesus and take refuge in Him.

—*Dennis DeHaan*

Psalm 3

¹O LORD, how many are my foes!
    How many rise up against me!
²Many are saying of me,
    "God will not deliver him."   *Selah*

³But you are a shield around me, O LORD;
    you bestow glory on me and lift up my head.
⁴To the LORD I cry aloud,
    and he answers me from his holy hill.   *Selah*

⁵I lie down and sleep;
    I wake again, because the LORD sustains me.
⁶I will not fear the tens of thousands
    drawn up against me on every side.

⁷Arise, O LORD!
    Deliver me, O my God!
  Strike all my enemies on the jaw;
    break the teeth of the wicked.
⁸From the LORD comes deliverance.
    May your blessing be on your people.   *Selah*

God, My Glory

Is God your glory? (Psalm 3:3). The word *glory* is the translation of a Hebrew word meaning "weight" or "significance."

Some people measure their worth by beauty, intelligence, money, power, or prestige. But David, who wrote Psalm 3, found his security and worth in God. He said that many stood against him. He heard their cruel voices and was tempted to believe them, to give way to discouragement and depression. Nevertheless, he comforted and strengthened his heart with these words: "But you are a shield around me, O LORD; you bestow glory on me and lift up my head" (v. 3).

What a change that realization made! He had God, and his enemies did not. So he could hold up his head with confidence.

Verses like Psalm 3:3 can bring peace to your heart even in the midst of a storm of trouble. God is your shield and deliverer. He will deal with your adversaries in due time.

Meanwhile, tell God all about your troubles. Let Him be your glory. You don't have to defend yourself. Ask Him to be your shield—to protect your heart with His overshadowing love and care. Then, like David, you can lie down in peace and sleep, though tens of thousands are against you (vv. 5–6).

—*David Roper*

Psalm 4

[1] Answer me when I call to you,
    O my righteous God.
  Give me relief from my distress;
    be merciful to me and hear my prayer.

[2] How long, O men, will you turn my glory into shame?
    How long will you love delusions and seek false gods?   *Selah*
[3] Know that the LORD has set apart the godly for himself;
    the LORD will hear when I call to him.

[4] In your anger do not sin;
    when you are on your beds,
    search your hearts and be silent.   *Selah*
[5] Offer right sacrifices
    and trust in the LORD.

[6] Many are asking, "Who can show us any good?"
    Let the light of your face shine upon us, O LORD.
[7] You have filled my heart with greater joy
    than when their grain and new wine abound.
[8] I will lie down and sleep in peace,
    for you alone, O LORD,
    make me dwell in safety.

Sleeping in Safety

Someone has said, "The rest of your life depends on the rest of your nights." Many people, though, feel like the little boy who was having trouble falling asleep. He told his mother, "My body is lying down, but my mind keeps sitting up!"

If anxious thoughts keep you awake, ask the Lord to quiet your heart and give you the faith to be able to relax and let Him solve the problems that disturb you. That's what David did when he was in trouble, for he wrote, "I will lie down and sleep in peace, for you alone, O LORD, make me dwell in safety" (Psalm 4:8). When you realize that your heavenly Father is watching over you, you can find sweet rest.

During World War II, an elderly woman in England had endured the nerve-shattering bombings with amazing serenity. When asked to give the secret of her calmness amid the terror and danger, she replied, "Well, every night I say my prayers. And then I remember that God is always watching, so I go peacefully to sleep. After all, there is no need for both of us to stay awake!"

Yes, you may not only sleep, but you can do so peacefully if you recognize that your heavenly Father is tenderly watching over you.

—*Henry Bosch*

Psalm 5

[1] Give ear to my words, O LORD,
   consider my sighing.
[2] Listen to my cry for help,
   my King and my God,
   for to you I pray.
[3] In the morning, O LORD, you hear my voice;
   in the morning I lay my requests before you
   and wait in expectation.

[4] You are not a God who takes pleasure in evil;
   with you the wicked cannot dwell.
[5] The arrogant cannot stand in your presence;
   you hate all who do wrong.
[6] You destroy those who tell lies;
   bloodthirsty and deceitful men
   the LORD abhors.

[7] But I, by your great mercy,
   will come into your house;
   in reverence will I bow down
   toward your holy temple.
[8] Lead me, O LORD, in your righteousness
   because of my enemies—
   make straight your way before me.

[9] Not a word from their mouth can be trusted;
   their heart is filled with destruction.
   Their throat is an open grave;
   with their tongue they speak deceit.
[10] Declare them guilty, O God!
   Let their intrigues be their downfall.
   Banish them for their many sins,
   for they have rebelled against you.
[11] But let all who take refuge in you be glad;
   let them ever sing for joy.
   Spread your protection over them,
   that those who love your name may rejoice in you.
[12] For surely, O LORD, you bless the righteous;
   you surround them with your favor as with a shield.

Seeing Jesus in the Morning

I heard about a little boy who didn't want to get out of bed one day. He told his parents, "I won't get up until I see Jesus." At first they didn't know what he meant. But when he pointed to a picture on the wall, which was a painting of Christ, they understood. He wouldn't get out of bed until it was light enough to see the face of Jesus.

That boy's remark reminds me that our first thoughts when we wake up to a new day should be directed to our Lord in heaven.

English preacher Joseph Parker said, "The morning is the time for meeting the Lord, for then we are at our best, having a new supply of energy. Blessed is the day that is opened with prayer! Holy is the dawn that finds us on 'top of the mount' with God!"

In the Old Testament, the Levites stood "every morning to thank and praise the LORD. They were to do the same in the evening" (1 Chronicles 23:30). According to the New Testament, all believers are priests (1 Peter 2:5, 9). We too have the privilege of communing daily with God.

What do you think about when you first wake up? Why not follow the practice of the psalmist who directed his prayer to God in the morning and looked to Him for strength? It's important to begin each day with Jesus.

—*Henry Bosch*

Psalm 6

¹O LORD, do not rebuke me in your anger
   or discipline me in your wrath.
²Be merciful to me, LORD, for I am faint;
   O LORD, heal me, for my bones are in agony.
³My soul is in anguish.
   How long, O LORD, how long?

⁴Turn, O LORD, and deliver me;
   save me because of your unfailing love.
⁵No one remembers you when he is dead.
   Who praises you from the grave?

⁶I am worn out from groaning;
   all night long I flood my bed with weeping
   and drench my couch with tears.
⁷My eyes grow weak with sorrow;
   they fail because of all my foes.

⁸Away from me, all you who do evil,
   for the LORD has heard my weeping.
⁹The LORD has heard my cry for mercy;
   the LORD accepts my prayer.
¹⁰All my enemies will be ashamed and dismayed;
   they will turn back in sudden disgrace.

Praying with Boldness

Have you ever found it tough to pray? That can happen when we're reluctant to tell God how we're really feeling. We might abruptly stop in mid-sentence, fearful of being disrespectful of our heavenly Father.

A trip through the book of Psalms can help us pray more openly. There we can overhear David's conversations with God and realize that he was not afraid to be completely open and honest with the Lord. David cried out: "O LORD, do not rebuke me in your anger" (Psalm 6:1). "Be merciful to me, LORD, for I am faint" (6:2). "Why, O LORD, do you stand far off?" (10:1). "Do not turn a deaf ear to me" (28:1). "Plead my cause, O LORD" (35:1 NKJV). "Hear my prayer, O God" (54:2). "My thoughts trouble me and I am distraught" (55:2).

Think about David's approach. He was saying to God: "Help me!" "Listen to me!" "Don't be mad at me!" "Where are You?" David boldly went to God and told Him what was on his mind. Yes, God expects us to come to Him with a clean heart, and we need to approach Him with reverence—but we don't have to be afraid to tell God what we're thinking and feeling.

Next time you talk with your heavenly Father, tell it straight. He'll listen, and He'll understand.

—*Dave Branon*

Psalm 8

[1] O LORD, our Lord,
   how majestic is your name in all the earth!

 You have set your glory
   above the heavens.
[2] From the lips of children and infants
   you have ordained praise
   because of your enemies,
   to silence the foe and the avenger.

[3] When I consider your heavens,
   the work of your fingers,
 the moon and the stars,
   which you have set in place,
[4] what is man that you are mindful of him,
   the son of man that you care for him?
[5] You made him a little lower than the heavenly beings
   and crowned him with glory and honor.

[6] You made him ruler over the works of your hands;
   you put everything under his feet:
[7] all flocks and herds,
   and the beasts of the field,
[8] the birds of the air,
   and the fish of the sea,
   all that swim the paths of the seas.

[9] O LORD, our Lord,
   how majestic is your name in all the earth!

Why We Have Value

In a commencement address to a graduating class at Miami University, columnist George Will gave some statistics that help to diminish our sense of self-importance. He pointed out that "the sun around which Earth orbits is one of perhaps 400 billion stars in the Milky Way, which is a piddling galaxy next door to nothing much." He added, "There are perhaps forty billion galaxies in the still-unfolding universe. If all the stars in the universe were only the size of the head of a pin, they still would fill Miami's Orange Bowl to overflowing more than three billion times."

There is a plus side to all that overwhelming data. The God who created and sustains our star-studded cosmos in its incomprehensible vastness loves us. And He doesn't just love the human race as an entity of multiplied billions. He loves us individually. What Paul exclaims to be true about himself is true about each of us in all our insignificance: Christ "loved me and gave himself for me" (Galatians 2:20).

Astronomically, we are insignificant. But we are the beloved objects of God's care. While we have no reason for pride, we are inexpressibly grateful to the Lord whose love for us personally is revealed at Calvary's cross.

—*Vernon Grounds*

Psalm 9:1–14

¹ I will praise you, O LORD, with all my heart;
    I will tell of all your wonders.
² I will be glad and rejoice in you;
    I will sing praise to your name, O Most High.

³ My enemies turn back;
    they stumble and perish before you.
⁴ For you have upheld my right and my cause;
    you have sat on your throne, judging righteously.
⁵ You have rebuked the nations and destroyed the wicked;
    you have blotted out their name for ever and ever.
⁶ Endless ruin has overtaken the enemy,
    you have uprooted their cities;
    even the memory of them has perished.

⁷ The LORD reigns forever;
    he has established his throne for judgment.
⁸ He will judge the world in righteousness;
    he will govern the peoples with justice.
⁹ The LORD is a refuge for the oppressed,
    a stronghold in times of trouble.
¹⁰ Those who know your name will trust in you,
    for you, LORD, have never forsaken those who seek you.

¹¹ Sing praises to the LORD, enthroned in Zion;
    proclaim among the nations what he has done.
¹² For he who avenges blood remembers;
    he does not ignore the cry of the afflicted.

¹³ O LORD, see how my enemies persecute me!
    Have mercy and lift me up from the gates of death,
¹⁴ that I may declare your praises
    in the gates of the Daughter of Zion
    and there rejoice in your salvation.

Dial 9 for Worship

You're in the dentist's office and it's taking longer than expected. You're late for another appointment, so you ask to use the phone. You dial the number twice and nothing happens. "How do I dial out?" you ask in frustration. "I'm sorry," says the receptionist, "you need to dial 9 first."

You've come to church to worship God. You're singing. You're praying along with the pastor and following the Bible passages as they are read. But nothing's happening inside. You want to worship the Lord, but you're just going through the motions. What can you do?

Here's a suggestion: Dial 9. Open your Bible to Psalm 9 and follow David's prompts as he expresses his heartfelt praise to the Lord.

- Open your heart (v. 1). Let praise roll forth!
- Review all the things He has done for you (v. 1).
- Rejoice! Be glad! Sing! (v. 2)
- Acknowledge that He defends you (vv. 3–5).
- Go to Him for refuge (v. 9).
- Talk about what He's done for you (v. 11).
- Receive His mercy and rejoice in His salvation (vv. 13–14).

Try following David's example. You'll reconnect with God in your worship and praise.

—Dave Egner

Psalm 13

1 How long, O LORD? Will you forget me forever?
    How long will you hide your face from me?
2 How long must I wrestle with my thoughts
    and every day have sorrow in my heart?
    How long will my enemy triumph over me?

3 Look on me and answer, O LORD my God.
    Give light to my eyes, or I will sleep in death;
4 my enemy will say, "I have overcome him,"
    and my foes will rejoice when I fall.

5 But I trust in your unfailing love;
    my heart rejoices in your salvation.
6 I will sing to the LORD,
    for he has been good to me.

How Long?

My friends Bob and Delores understand what it means to wait for answers—answers that never seem to come. When their son Jason and future daughter-in-law Lindsay were murdered in August 2004, a national manhunt was undertaken to find the killer and bring him to justice. After two years of prayer and pursuit, there were still no tangible answers to the painful questions the two hurting families wrestled with. There was only silence.

In such times, we are vulnerable to wrong assumptions and conclusions about life, about God, and about prayer. In Psalm 13, David wrestled with the problem of unanswered prayer. He questioned why the world was so dangerous and pleaded for answers from God.

It's a hard psalm that David sang, and it seems to be one of frustration. Yet, in the end, his doubts and fears turned to trust. Why? Because the circumstances of our struggles cannot diminish the character of God and His care for His children. In verse 5, David turned a corner. From his heart he prayed, "But I trust in your unfailing love; my heart rejoices in your salvation."

In the pain and struggle of living without answers, we can always find comfort in our heavenly Father.

—*Bill Crowder*

Psalm 14

¹The fool says in his heart,
    "There is no God."
They are corrupt, their deeds are vile;
    there is no one who does good.

²The LORD looks down from heaven
    on the sons of men
to see if there are any who understand,
    any who seek God.
³All have turned aside,
    they have together become corrupt;
there is no one who does good,
    not even one.

⁴Will evildoers never learn—
    those who devour my people as men eat bread
    and who do not call on the LORD?
⁵There they are, overwhelmed with dread,
    for God is present in the company of the righteous.
⁶You evildoers frustrate the plans of the poor,
    but the LORD is their refuge.

⁷Oh, that salvation for Israel would come out of Zion!
    When the LORD restores the fortunes of his people,
    let Jacob rejoice and Israel be glad!

Say the Word

People seldom use the word *sin* any more. When we do something wrong, we say we showed "inappropriate behavior" or made a "tactical error" or "mistake." We may even say, "I have done a bad thing." It seems as if people have come to believe in their own innate goodness.

We do so in spite of overwhelming physical and spiritual evidence to the contrary. Genocide has been rampant in Sudan. Unbelievable atrocities have been endured in Bosnia and Rwanda. Who can forget the killing fields of Cambodia? And what about the millions of unborn babies killed in the United States in the name of convenience? Evil has not dropped off the face of the earth.

As followers of Jesus, we must steadfastly resist the efforts of our world to minimize the reality of sin. We must agree with God that "there is no one who does good, not even one" (Psalm 14:3).

Recognizing the sins of nations is easier than admitting our own personal sin. But we need to confess the specific sins we commit against our holy God. "If we claim we have not sinned, we make him out to be a liar and his word has no place in our lives" (1 John 1:10).

Call your sin "sin" and confess it to God.

—Dave Egner

Psalm 15

¹LORD, who may dwell in your sanctuary?
    Who may live on your holy hill?
²He whose walk is blameless
    and who does what is righteous,
  who speaks the truth from his heart
³and has no slander on his tongue,
 who does his neighbor no wrong
    and casts no slur on his fellowman,
⁴who despises a vile man
    but honors those who fear the LORD,
 who keeps his oath
    even when it hurts,
⁵who lends his money without usury
    and does not accept a bribe against the innocent.
 He who does these things
    will never be shaken.

What Did You Say?

At Santa Clara University in California, a researcher conducted a study of 1,500 business managers that revealed what workers value most in a supervisor. Employees said they respected a leader who shows competence, has the ability to inspire workers, and is skillful in providing direction.

But there was a fourth quality they admired even more—integrity. Above all else, workers wanted a manager whose word was good, one who was known for his honesty, and one whom they could trust.

While this finding holds special significance for Christian managers, it also says something to everyone who claims to be a follower of Jesus. Integrity should characterize all believers, no matter what their position may be.

According to Psalm 15, truth is at the heart of every word and deed of a godly person. Since the God of the Bible always keeps His word, it follows that a godly person will be known as one who does what he says he will do.

We all need to be more careful about our integrity. Do those around us admire us for our honesty? Does the Lord see us faithfully doing what we said we would do—even when it hurts? (Psalm 15:4).

—*Mart DeHaan*

Psalm 17:1–9

[1] Hear, O LORD, my righteous plea;
    listen to my cry.
  Give ear to my prayer—
    it does not rise from deceitful lips.
[2] May my vindication come from you;
    may your eyes see what is right.

[3] Though you probe my heart and examine me at night,
    though you test me, you will find nothing;
    I have resolved that my mouth will not sin.
[4] As for the deeds of men—
    by the word of your lips
    I have kept myself
    from the ways of the violent.
[5] My steps have held to your paths;
    my feet have not slipped.

[6] I call on you, O God, for you will answer me;
    give ear to me and hear my prayer.
[7] Show the wonder of your great love,
    you who save by your right hand
    those who take refuge in you from their foes.
[8] Keep me as the apple of your eye;
    hide me in the shadow of your wings
[9] from the wicked who assail me,
    from my mortal enemies who surround me.

Refuge Needed

In the aftermath of Hurricane Katrina's devastation of the southern United States, displaced families and individuals were often referred to in the media as "refugees." For some, this term was viewed as insulting, so it prompted reporters to scramble for another word that would not be perceived as negative. They decided on the word *evacuees*.

In actuality, the word *refugee* is filled with hope. One dictionary defines it as "one who flees in search of refuge, as in times of war, political oppression, or religious persecution." Refugee comes from the word *refuge*, which speaks of safety, protection, and care for the hurting. It speaks of a safe haven in a storm-filled world.

For those who have been battered by the storms, tragedies, and disasters of life, refuge is what they long for most. They may seek shelter in the arms of God, who alone can give us refuge and who longs to cover us and protect us and preserve us.

Jesus said to the broken people of His day, "How often I have longed to gather your children together, as a hen gathers her chicks under her wings" (Matthew 23:37). He continues to offer refuge to the hurting hearts of our day if we will but seek His care and trust His heart.

—*Bill Crowder*

Psalm 18:1–6

[1] I love you, O LORD, my strength.

[2] The LORD is my rock, my fortress and my deliverer;
    my God is my rock, in whom I take refuge.
    He is my shield and the horn of my salvation, my stronghold.
[3] I call to the LORD, who is worthy of praise,
    and I am saved from my enemies.

[4] The cords of death entangled me;
    the torrents of destruction overwhelmed me.
[5] The cords of the grave coiled around me;
    the snares of death confronted me.
[6] In my distress I called to the LORD;
    I cried to my God for help.
  From his temple he heard my voice;
    my cry came before him, into his ears.

The Lord Is My Rock

It turns out that we humans reason largely by means of our hearts and not by our heads. As French mathematician and theologian Blaise Pascal noted long ago, "The heart has reasons that reason does not know."

Poets, singers, storytellers, and artists have always known this. They use symbols and metaphors that speak to our hearts rather than to our minds. That's why their ideas penetrate where everything else has failed. And that's why we say, "A picture is worth a thousand words." Images remain in our minds when all else is forgotten.

David wrote, "The LORD is my rock, my fortress . . . my shield and the horn of my salvation, my stronghold" (Psalm 18:2). He was thinking of physical elements that convey spiritual realities. Each picture expresses a deeper thought, linking the visible world to the invisible realm of the Spirit. David doesn't wander into definition and explanation, for explanation can blunt imagination. Each picture is left hanging in our minds—images that evoke mystery, arouse our imagination, and deepen our understanding.

David wakes up what is hidden deep within us. It's good to think long thoughts about it. What does this mean to you: God is my rock, my fortress, my shield?

—*David Roper*

Psalm 19:1–6

[1] The heavens declare the glory of God;
  the skies proclaim the work of his hands.
[2] Day after day they pour forth speech;
  night after night they display knowledge.
[3] There is no speech or language
  where their voice is not heard.
[4] Their voice goes out into all the earth,
  their words to the ends of the world.

In the heavens he has pitched a tent for the sun,
[5] which is like a bridegroom coming forth from his pavilion,
  like a champion rejoicing to run his course.
[6] It rises at one end of the heavens
  and makes its circuit to the other;
  nothing is hidden from its heat.

Message from the Sky

The earth's population is now over 6.6 billion. And depending on where we live, finding moments of solitude where we can gaze at the silent night sky is increasingly difficult. Yet, according to the writer of Psalm 19, if we were able to steal away to a spot where the only sound was our heartbeat and the only sight the canopy of the stars, we could hear a message from those heavens.

In such a moment, we could hear with the ears of our innermost being the noiseless testimony of God's breathtaking creation.

We could hear from the heavens as they "declare the glory of God" (v. 1). And we could watch in amazement as the skies "proclaim the work of his hands" (v. 1).

We could listen as "day after day they pour forth speech" that fills our minds with the unmistakable awareness of God's splendid creation (v. 2).

We could marvel through the night as the firmament shows in unmistakable splendor the knowledge of God's handiwork (vv. 1–2).

Our Creator tells us to "be still, and know that I am God" (Psalm 46:10). A great way to do this is to spend time in His creation admiring His handiwork. Then we will certainly know that He is God!

—*Dave Branon*

Psalm 20

¹ May the LORD answer you when you are in distress;
　　may the name of the God of Jacob protect you.
² May he send you help from the sanctuary
　　and grant you support from Zion.
³ May he remember all your sacrifices
　　and accept your burnt offerings.　*Selah*
⁴ May he give you the desire of your heart
　　and make all your plans succeed.
⁵ We will shout for joy when you are victorious
　　and will lift up our banners in the name of our God.
　May the LORD grant all your requests.

⁶ Now I know that the LORD saves his anointed;
　　he answers him from his holy heaven
　　with the saving power of his right hand.
⁷ Some trust in chariots and some in horses,
　　but we trust in the name of the LORD our God.
⁸ They are brought to their knees and fall,
　　but we rise up and stand firm.

⁹ O LORD, save the king!
　　Answer us when we call!

Protect Us by Thy Might

Every year on July 4, Americans celebrate Independence Day. Other countries have their own special days for commemorating their nation's birth.

French writer Alexis de Tocqueville, after visiting America in 1831, said, "I sought for the greatness of the United States in her commodious harbors, her ample rivers, her fertile fields, and boundless forests—and it was not there. I sought for it in her rich mines, her vast world commerce, her public school system, and in her institutions of higher learning—and it was not there. I looked for it in her democratic Congress and her matchless Constitution—and it was not there. Not until I went into the churches of America and heard her pulpits flame with righteousness did I understand the secret of her genius and power. America is great because America is good, and if America ever ceases to be good, America will cease to be great!"

If any land is to be free, its citizens must acknowledge with the psalmist, "We trust in the name of the Lord our God!" They must not trust in massive armaments, material wealth, or scientific progress. Many nations have done this, only to be destroyed.

History bears silent witness to this truth: No nation can stand that refuses to trust in God.

—*Henry Bosch*

Psalm 23

[1] The LORD is my shepherd, I shall not be in want.
[2] He makes me lie down in green pastures,
he leads me beside quiet waters,
[3] he restores my soul.
He guides me in paths of righteousness
for his name's sake.
[4] Even though I walk
through the valley of the shadow of death,
I will fear no evil,
for you are with me;
your rod and your staff,
they comfort me.

[5] You prepare a table before me
in the presence of my enemies.
You anoint my head with oil;
my cup overflows.
[6] Surely goodness and love will follow me
all the days of my life,
and I will dwell in the house of the LORD
forever.

Another Walk with Whitaker

My dog Whitaker and I like to take early-morning walks through the woods. He runs ahead while I amble along, meditating or praying. I know where we're going; he's not sure. I stay on the trail and he trots ahead—sniffing, investigating, and taking occasional forays into the forest to chase real or imagined chipmunks.

Though Whit is ahead, I'm leading. Every so often he checks to see where I am. If I've turned back toward home or gone on to another trail, I hear his pounding feet and panting breath as he races to catch up with me. If I hide behind some brush, he runs to the last place he saw me and tracks me down. Then we walk the trail together again.

It's like that with God's leading. He knows the way because He has prepared the way. But sometimes we may not see Him—so we do our best to go where He wants by following the guidance of His Word. Other times it may seem as if He is hidden from us. His pace may not be as fast as we would like, or we wish He would slow down.

Just as Whitaker keeps looking back at me, we need to look to God and His Word at every juncture we come to. We must rely on the direction of His Spirit.

That's what I thought about today while I was walking with Whitaker.

—*Dave Egner*

Psalm 24

¹ The earth is the LORD's, and everything in it,
    the world, and all who live in it;
² for he founded it upon the seas
    and established it upon the waters.
³ Who may ascend the hill of the LORD?
    Who may stand in his holy place?
⁴ He who has clean hands and a pure heart,
    who does not lift up his soul to an idol
    or swear by what is false.
⁵ He will receive blessing from the LORD
    and vindication from God his Savior.
⁶ Such is the generation of those who seek him,
    who seek your face, O God of Jacob.   *Selah*

⁷ Lift up your heads, O you gates;
    be lifted up, you ancient doors,
    that the King of glory may come in.
⁸ Who is this King of glory?
    The LORD strong and mighty,
    the LORD mighty in battle.
⁹ Lift up your heads, O you gates;
    lift them up, you ancient doors,
    that the King of glory may come in.
¹⁰ Who is he, this King of glory?
    The LORD Almighty—
    he is the King of glory.   *Selah*

A Selah Moment

King David proclaimed: "The LORD Almighty—he is the King of glory" (Psalm 24:10). The word *Selah* was later added to the end of this psalm and many others. Some believe it refers to an instrumental interlude because the psalms were often set to music. Biblical scholars also suggest other possible meanings, including "silence," "pause," "interruption," "accentuate," "exalt," or "end."

Reflecting on these words can help us to take a *"Selah* moment" to pause and worship God during the day.

Be silent and listen to the voice of God (Psalm 46:10).

Pause from a hectic schedule to be refreshed in spirit (Psalm 42:1–2).

Interrupt the day to do a spiritual inventory and be cleansed (Psalm 51:1–10).

Accentuate the joy of God's provision through thanksgiving (Psalm 65:9–13).

Exalt the name of God for answered prayer in spite of disappointment (Psalm 40:1–3).

End the day by reflecting on the Lord's faithfulness (Psalm 119:148).

David's reflection on God included a *Selah* moment. Following his example will help us worship our God throughout the day.

—Dennis Fisher

Psalm 25:1–10

[1] To you, O LORD, I lift up my soul;
[2] in you I trust, O my God.
  Do not let me be put to shame,
      nor let my enemies triumph over me.
[3] No one whose hope is in you
      will ever be put to shame,
  but they will be put to shame
      who are treacherous without excuse.

[4] Show me your ways, O LORD,
      teach me your paths;
[5] guide me in your truth and teach me,
      for you are God my Savior,
      and my hope is in you all day long.
[6] Remember, O LORD, your great mercy and love,
      for they are from of old.
[7] Remember not the sins of my youth
      and my rebellious ways;
  according to your love remember me,
      for you are good, O LORD.
[8] Good and upright is the LORD;
      therefore he instructs sinners in his ways.
[9] He guides the humble in what is right
      and teaches them his way.
[10] All the ways of the LORD are loving and faithful
      for those who keep the demands of his covenant.

Riding Out the Waves

What can ride ocean currents for years before finally washing ashore and springing to life? According to *National Geographic World* magazine, it's a nut that is native to South America and the West Indies. Some people call them "sea hearts."

These two-inch, chestnut-colored nuts are hardy, heart-shaped seeds that grow on high-climbing vines. They often fall into rivers and float out to sea. There they may ride the currents for years before coming to shore and sprouting into a plant.

This life-bearing, time-enduring, wave-riding seed illustrates a basic spiritual principle. God's plans may include extended times of waiting for Him to act on our behalf. This was true of Noah, who endured ridicule while spending 120 years building a ship; of Abraham, who waited for the fulfillment of God's promise that he would have a son in his old age; and of David, God's anointed, who chose to wait for God's timing rather than take the life of envious King Saul.

Sea hearts can't choose to be patient, but we can. Nothing is harder or better for us than to follow the example of David, who wrote Psalm 25. By waiting on the Lord we can have peace, and our faith will grow—even while we are riding out the waves.

—*Mart DeHaan*

Psalm 26

¹Vindicate me, O LORD,
    For I have walked in my integrity.
    I have also trusted in the LORD;
    I shall not slip.
²Examine me, O LORD, and prove me;
    Try my mind and my heart.
³For Your lovingkindness is before my eyes,
    And I have walked in Your truth.
⁴I have not sat with idolatrous mortals,
    Nor will I go in with hypocrites.
⁵I have hated the assembly of evildoers,
    And will not sit with the wicked.

⁶I will wash my hands in innocence;
    So I will go about Your altar, O LORD,
⁷That I may proclaim with the voice of thanksgiving,
    And tell of all Your wondrous works.
⁸LORD, I have loved the habitation of Your house,
    And the place where Your glory dwells.

⁹Do not gather my soul with sinners,
    Nor my life with bloodthirsty men,
¹⁰In whose hands is a sinister scheme
    And whose right hand is full of bribes.

¹¹But as for me, I will walk in my integrity;
    Redeem me and be merciful to me.
¹²My foot stands in an even place
    In the congregations I will bless the LORD.

                       (NKJV)

Dealing with Self-Doubt

Sometimes, when I've been falsely accused, I have found myself questioning my sincerity. When I do, I follow the example of David in Psalm 26 as he responded to his critics.

Appealing directly to the Lord, he expressed his firm conviction that he had walked in "integrity" (the Hebrew word means sincerity, not faultlessness). He asked God to vindicate him, for he had renounced the ways of the wicked, declared his love for God's temple, and pleaded for deliverance from the fate of the ungodly (vv. 1–10). Finally, he reaffirmed his resolve to live with sincerity, humbly asked God to redeem him, and acknowledged his need for mercy (v. 11).

What happened next? God gave David the assurance that he stood in "an even place" (v. 12), a symbolic way of saying he was in a place of safety, accepted and protected by the Lord. As a result, he closed his psalm on a note of confidence and anticipation.

Have the painful barbs of critics or the accusations of your conscience filled you with fear and self-doubt? Talk to the Lord. If you need to confess sin, do it. Then put your hope and trust in God. He will replace your insecurity and doubt with His supernatural peace. He has done that for me. He will do the same for you.

—Herb VanderLugt

Psalm 27:1–6, 13–14

[1] The LORD is my light and my salvation—
  whom shall I fear?
The LORD is the stronghold of my life—
  of whom shall I be afraid?
[2] When evil men advance against me
  to devour my flesh,
when my enemies and my foes attack me,
  they will stumble and fall.
[3] Though an army besiege me,
  my heart will not fear;
though war break out against me,
  even then will I be confident.

[4] One thing I ask of the LORD,
  this is what I seek:
that I may dwell in the house of the LORD
  all the days of my life,
to gaze upon the beauty of the LORD
  and to seek him in his temple.
[5] For in the day of trouble
  he will keep me safe in his dwelling;
he will hide me in the shelter of his tabernacle
  and set me high upon a rock.
[6] Then my head will be exalted
  above the enemies who surround me;
at his tabernacle will I sacrifice with shouts of joy;
  I will sing and make music to the LORD.

[13] I am still confident of this:
  I will see the goodness of the LORD
  in the land of the living.
[14] Wait for the LORD;
  be strong and take heart
  and wait for the LORD.

Facing Your Enemies

During the United States Civil War, fierce fighting was taking place near Moorefield, West Virginia. Because the town was close to enemy lines, it would be controlled one day by Union troops and the next by Confederates.

In the heart of the town lived an old woman. According to the testimony of a Presbyterian minister, one morning several enemy soldiers knocked on her door and demanded breakfast. She asked them in and said she would prepare something for them.

When the food was ready, she said, "It's my custom to read the Bible and pray before breakfast. I hope you won't mind." They consented, so she took her Bible, opened it at random, and began to read Psalm 27. "The LORD is my light and my salvation—whom shall I fear? The LORD is the stronghold of my life—of whom shall I be afraid?" (v. 1). She read on through the last verse: "Wait for the LORD; be strong and take heart and wait for the LORD" (v. 14). When she finished reading, she said, "Let us pray." While she was praying, she heard sounds of the men moving around in the room. When she said "amen" and looked up, the soldiers were gone.

Meditate on Psalm 27. If you are facing enemies, God will use His Word to help you.

—*Haddon Robinson*

Psalm 28

[1] To you I call, O LORD my Rock;
    do not turn a deaf ear to me.
  For if you remain silent,
    I will be like those who have gone down to the pit.
[2] Hear my cry for mercy
    as I call to you for help,
  as I lift up my hands
    toward your Most Holy Place.

[3] Do not drag me away with the wicked,
    with those who do evil,
  who speak cordially with their neighbors
    but harbor malice in their hearts.
[4] Repay them for their deeds
    and for their evil work;
  repay them for what their hands have done
    and bring back upon them what they deserve.
[5] Since they show no regard for the works of the LORD
    and what his hands have done,
  he will tear them down
    and never build them up again.

[6] Praise be to the LORD,
    for he has heard my cry for mercy.
[7] The LORD is my strength and my shield;
    my heart trusts in him, and I am helped.
  My heart leaps for joy
    and I will give thanks to him in song.

[8] The LORD is the strength of his people,
    a fortress of salvation for his anointed one.
[9] Save your people and bless your inheritance;
    be their shepherd and carry them forever.

How Strong Is Your Song?

A lark will not sing while perched on its nest. But when it leaves and begins to wing its way toward the sky, you'll hear its lovely song. The higher the bird ascends, the louder and sweeter its music becomes. You can always tell when it begins to descend, because its joyful melody gets softer and softer. The closer the lark comes to earth, the less it sings. At last when it returns to its nest, its music ceases altogether.

We too have no song of victory in our heart as long as we restrict our thoughts to the nest of our old sinful nature and to the depressing circumstances of our earthly existence. As we think of our own weakness and all the evil in the world, we can become overwhelmed and disheartened. However, as we meditate on our exalted standing in Christ and draw near to God, we discover that He draws near to us (James 4:8). The happiness that springs from this close fellowship invigorates our soul. The more we rely on Him, the more we grow in grace and spiritual understanding. We learn to depend on the indwelling Holy Spirit, and we find that the joy of the Lord is our strength (Nehemiah 8:10).

Let's center our attention on the Lord and all He is doing for us instead of thinking about our own weak self and our disturbing circumstances. He will lift us above them and help us gain a new perspective. Then we'll be able to "praise God's name in song" and "glorify him with thanksgiving" (Psalm 69:30).

—*Henry Bosch*

Psalm 30:4–12

4 Sing to the LORD, you saints of his;
    praise his holy name.
5 For his anger lasts only a moment,
    but his favor lasts a lifetime;
weeping may remain for a night,
    but rejoicing comes in the morning.

6 When I felt secure, I said,
    "I will never be shaken."
7 O LORD, when you favored me,
    you made my mountain stand firm;
but when you hid your face,
    I was dismayed.

8 To you, O LORD, I called;
    to the Lord I cried for mercy:
9 "What gain is there in my destruction,
    in my going down into the pit?
Will the dust praise you?
    Will it proclaim your faithfulness?
10 Hear, O LORD, and be merciful to me;
    O LORD, be my help."

11 You turned my wailing into dancing;
    you removed my sackcloth and clothed me with joy,
12 that my heart may sing to you and not be silent.
    O LORD my God, I will give you thanks forever.

Always Winter

Unlike some of my family—who can't wait to go down-hill skiing—I don't look forward to winter. When the first snowflake falls, I immediately start calculating how many months of Michigan winter are left.

Imagine C. S. Lewis's fictional world of Narnia, where for a hundred years it was always winter. Cold, wet snow—with no hope of springtime ever arriving to wipe away the memories of icy temperatures and piles of white stuff. But worst of all, in Narnia, Christmas never came. Always winter and never Christmas! To me, the best part of winter is the anticipation, excitement, and wonder of Christmas. Life is bleak when you have nothing to look forward to.

There are some whose souls are locked in winter. The hardness of life has frozen their hearts. Disappointed with life, they find that each day is filled with despair. "Weeping may remain for a night," the psalmist tells us, "but rejoicing comes in the morning" (Psalm 30:5). In the darkest times of our lives, God longs to turn our "wailing into dancing" (v. 11).

David wrote, "When anxiety was great within me, your consolation brought joy to my soul" (Psalm 94:19). If you cry out to God in the midst of your "winter," you can experience the joy of the Christ of Christmas today.

—*Cindy Hess Kasper*

Psalm 31:9–10, 14–18, 21–24

9 Be merciful to me, O LORD, for I am in distress;
 my eyes grow weak with sorrow,
 my soul and my body with grief.
10 My life is consumed by anguish
 and my years by groaning;
my strength fails because of my affliction,
 and my bones grow weak.

14 But I trust in you, O LORD;
 I say, "You are my God."
15 My times are in your hands;
 deliver me from my enemies
 and from those who pursue me.
16 Let your face shine on your servant;
 save me in your unfailing love.
17 Let me not be put to shame, O LORD,
 for I have cried out to you;
but let the wicked be put to shame
 and lie silent in the grave.
18 Let their lying lips be silenced,
 for with pride and contempt
 they speak arrogantly against the righteous.

21 Praise be to the LORD,
 for he showed his wonderful love to me
 when I was in a besieged city.
22 In my alarm I said,
 "I am cut off from your sight!"
Yet you heard my cry for mercy
 when I called to you for help.

23 Love the LORD, all his saints!
 The LORD preserves the faithful,
 but the proud he pays back in full.
24 Be strong and take heart,
 all you who hope in the LORD.

No Terror

After the terrorist bombing in Bali in 2002, one man reacted by giving up traveling. Three years later, he finally took his family for a holiday in Bali, together with fifty tourists from Newcastle, Australia. The trip ended in tragedy when his family was caught in a suicide bombing at a café on Jimbaran Beach.

From New York to Indonesia, warnings and threats of terrorist attacks continue. Terrorism derives its sting by exporting fear. No one feels safe.

In Psalm 31, David was in the grip of surrounding threats that terrorized both his reputation and his life. He wrote, "There is terror on every side," and said, "They . . . plot to take my life" (v. 13). When everything seemed bleakest, David cried in despair, "I trust in you, O LORD" (v. 14). He began to find peace when he acknowledged, "My times are in your hands" (v. 15).

In our world, perfect safety is not possible. But David's God is our God. Though our earthly security may be threatened, we can never lose God's eternal, unfailing love.

To those who trust in the Lord, David wrote these hope-filled words: "Be strong and take heart, all you who hope in the LORD" (v. 24). When we place our times in His hand, we can exchange the fear of terror for peace and praise.

—*Albert Lee*

Psalm 32

[1] Blessed is he
    whose transgressions are forgiven,
    whose sins are covered.
[2] Blessed is the man
    whose sin the LORD does not count against him
    and in whose spirit is no deceit.

[3] When I kept silent,
    my bones wasted away
    through my groaning all day long.
[4] For day and night
    your hand was heavy upon me;
    my strength was sapped
    as in the heat of summer.   *Selah*
[5] Then I acknowledged my sin to you
    and did not cover up my iniquity.
I said, "I will confess
    my transgressions to the LORD" —
and you forgave
    the guilt of my sin.   *Selah*

[6] Therefore let everyone who is godly pray to you
    while you may be found;
surely when the mighty waters rise,
    they will not reach him.
[7] You are my hiding place;
    you will protect me from trouble
    and surround me with songs of deliverance.   *Selah*

[8] I will instruct you and teach you in the way you should go;
    I will counsel you and watch over you.

Instincts

Flying into a storm is a dangerous experience. The temptation is to fly by your instincts, or, as aviators say, "by the seat of your pants." But as any pilot will tell you, that's a prescription for disaster. If you rely on your feelings and instincts, you become disoriented, thinking the plane is going up when it's actually going down. Thankfully, the instrument panel is set to magnetic north and can be trusted every time. Letting your instruments guide you, even when it feels like they're wrong, helps ensure safety in the storm.

We all face storms that threaten to confuse and disorient us. It may be a call from the doctor's office, a friend who has betrayed you, or a shattered dream. Those are the times to be especially careful. When you are blinded by life's disappointments, don't trust your instincts. Flying by the seat of your pants in the storms of life can lead to despair, confusion, and vengeful responses that make matters worse. God wants to guide you, and His Word is packed with wisdom and insights for living. His "word is a lamp to my feet and a light for my path" (Psalm 119:105). Where He leads is always right!

Go to your Bible, and trust God to guide you. He promises, "I will instruct you and teach you in the way you should go" (Psalm 32:8).

—*Joe Stowell*

Psalm 33:1–11

[1] Sing joyfully to the LORD, you righteous;
  it is fitting for the upright to praise him.
[2] Praise the LORD with the harp;
  make music to him on the ten-stringed lyre.
[3] Sing to him a new song;
  play skillfully, and shout for joy.

[4] For the word of the LORD is right and true;
  he is faithful in all he does.
[5] The LORD loves righteousness and justice;
  the earth is full of his unfailing love.

[6] By the word of the LORD were the heavens made,
  their starry host by the breath of his mouth.
[7] He gathers the waters of the sea into jars;
  he puts the deep into storehouses.
[8] Let all the earth fear the LORD;
  let all the people of the world revere him.
[9] For he spoke, and it came to be;
  he commanded, and it stood firm.
[10] The LORD foils the plans of the nations;
  he thwarts the purposes of the peoples.
[11] But the plans of the LORD stand firm forever,
  the purposes of his heart through all generations.

A New Song

I was walking in the park one morning, listening to a tape by the Brooklyn Tabernacle Choir. I had my ancient Walkman clipped to my belt and my headphones clamped over my ears, tuned in to another world. The music was joyous! Oblivious to my surroundings, I began to sing and dance.

Then I spied my neighbor, leaning against a tree with a bemused look on her face. She couldn't hear my music, but she was delighted by my behavior. I wish she could have heard my song.

I thought afterward of the new song God has placed in our hearts, a song we hear from another world. It tells us that God loves us and always will and that He has "rescued us from the dominion of darkness" (Colossians 1:13) and "seated us with him in the heavenly realms in Christ Jesus" (Ephesians 2:6). And someday He'll take us to be with Him forever.

In the meantime He has given us eternally useful things to do. Grace now and glory ahead! Is this not a reason to sing?

Next time you're down in the dumps, think about God's goodness. Tune in to the music of heaven and sing a new song with the angels. It may set your feet to dancing and cause great wonderment in those around you. Perhaps they'll want to hear the music too.

—David Roper

Psalm 34:11–22

11 Come, my children, listen to me;
   I will teach you the fear of the LORD.
12 Whoever of you loves life
   and desires to see many good days,
13 keep your tongue from evil
   and your lips from speaking lies.
14 Turn from evil and do good;
   seek peace and pursue it.

15 The eyes of the LORD are on the righteous
   and his ears are attentive to their cry;
16 the face of the LORD is against those who do evil,
   to cut off the memory of them from the earth.
17 The righteous cry out, and the LORD hears them;
   he delivers them from all their troubles.
18 The LORD is close to the brokenhearted
   and saves those who are crushed in spirit.
19 A righteous man may have many troubles,
   but the LORD delivers him from them all;
20 he protects all his bones,
   not one of them will be broken.

21 Evil will slay the wicked;
   the foes of the righteous will be condemned.
22 The LORD redeems his servants;
   no one will be condemned who takes refuge in him.

Rock Solid

It was a sad day in May 2003 when "The Old Man of the Mountain" broke apart and slid down the mountainside. This 40-foot profile of an old man's face, carved by nature in the White Mountains of New Hampshire, had long been an attraction to tourists, a solid presence for residents, and the official state emblem. It was written about by Nathaniel Hawthorne in his short story "The Great Stone Face."

Some nearby residents were devastated when the Old Man fell. One woman said, "I grew up thinking that someone was watching over me. I feel a little less watched-over now."

There are times when a dependable presence disappears. Something or someone we've relied on is gone, and our life is shaken. Maybe it's the loss of a loved one or a job or good health. The loss makes us feel off-balance, unstable. We might even think that God is no longer watching over us.

But "the eyes of the LORD are on the righteous and his ears are attentive to their cry" (Psalm 34:15). He "is close to the brokenhearted" (v. 18). He is the Rock on whose presence we can always depend (Deuteronomy 32:4).

God's presence is real. He continually watches over us. He is rock solid.

—*Anne Cetas*

Psalm 36

¹ An oracle is within my heart
   concerning the sinfulness of the wicked:
 There is no fear of God
   before his eyes.
² For in his own eyes he flatters himself
   too much to detect or hate his sin.
³ The words of his mouth are wicked and deceitful;
   he has ceased to be wise and to do good.
⁴ Even on his bed he plots evil;
   he commits himself to a sinful course
   and does not reject what is wrong.

⁵ Your love, O LORD, reaches to the heavens,
   your faithfulness to the skies.
⁶ Your righteousness is like the mighty mountains,
   your justice like the great deep.
 O LORD, you preserve both man and beast.
⁷ How priceless is your unfailing love!
 Both high and low among men
   find refuge in the shadow of your wings.
⁸ They feast on the abundance of your house;
   you give them drink from your river of delights.
⁹ For with you is the fountain of life;
   in your light we see light.

¹⁰ Continue your love to those who know you,
   your righteousness to the upright in heart.
¹¹ May the foot of the proud not come against me,
   nor the hand of the wicked drive me away.
¹² See how the evildoers lie fallen—
   thrown down, not able to rise!

God's Little Blessings

Our family was at Disney World a few years ago when God handed us one of His little blessings. Disney World is a huge place—107 acres huge, to be exact. You could walk around for days without seeing someone you know. My wife and I decided to do our own thing while our children sought out the really cool stuff. We parted at 9:00 a.m. and were planning a rendezvous around 6:00 p.m.

At about 2:00 p.m., my wife and I got a craving for tacos. We looked at our map and made our way to a Spanish-sounding place for Mexican food. We had just sat down with our food when we heard, "Hi, Mom. Hi, Dad." Our three amigos had, at the same time, a hankering for a hot burrito.

Ten minutes after they joined us, a violent summer storm ripped through the park with whipping winds, heavy rain, and loud thunder. My wife commented, "I'd be a wreck if the kids weren't with us during this!" It seemed that God had orchestrated our meeting.

Ever notice those blessings from Him? Ever spend time thanking Him for His concern and care? Consider how remarkable it is that the One who created the universe cares enough to intervene in your life. "How priceless is your unfailing love," O God!

—*Dave Branon*

Psalm 37:23–31

²³ If the LORD delights in a man's way,
    he makes his steps firm;
²⁴ though he stumble, he will not fall,
    for the LORD upholds him with his hand.

²⁵ I was young and now I am old,
    yet I have never seen the righteous forsaken
    or their children begging bread.
²⁶ They are always generous and lend freely;
    their children will be blessed.

²⁷ Turn from evil and do good;
    then you will dwell in the land forever.
²⁸ For the LORD loves the just
    and will not forsake his faithful ones.

They will be protected forever,
    but the offspring of the wicked will be cut off;
²⁹ the righteous will inherit the land
    and dwell in it forever.

³⁰ The mouth of the righteous man utters wisdom,
    and his tongue speaks what is just.
³¹ The law of his God is in his heart;
    his feet do not slip.

No Longer Young

Recently, as I left a shop, I overheard the man who had served me whisper in disappointment, "He called me 'uncle,' when he's definitely older than I am."

Since childhood, my Chinese culture has taught me it is polite to say, "Thank you, Uncle!" for help received. This gesture has served me well, but now I have to think twice before using it. Taking a good look in the mirror, my eyes confirm that I am no longer the person my mind remembers.

Being young has many advantages, but with age comes the joy of reflecting on God's faithfulness. David reminds us in Psalm 37: "I was young and now I am old, yet I have never seen the righteous forsaken" (v. 25).

Now that I'm in my fifties, I reflect and wonder how I ever could have thought that God had forsaken me. Yes, He has permitted me to face what seemed like insurmountable difficulties, but now I know it was only to shape me. God has always preserved me, and when I stumble I know it is "the Lord [who] upholds [me] with his hand" (v. 24).

We are growing older all the time, but we can also grow more thankful for God's many mercies. Above all, we are grateful that He puts the love of His law in our hearts and keeps our steps from slipping (v. 31).

—Albert Lee

Psalm 39:1–11, 13

¹I said, "I will watch my ways
  and keep my tongue from sin;
 I will put a muzzle on my mouth
  as long as the wicked are in my presence."
²But when I was silent and still,
  not even saying anything good,
  my anguish increased.
³My heart grew hot within me,
  and as I meditated, the fire burned;
  then I spoke with my tongue:

⁴"Show me, O LORD, my life's end
  and the number of my days;
  let me know how fleeting is my life.
⁵You have made my days a mere handbreadth;
  the span of my years is as nothing before you.
  Each man's life is but a breath.   *Selah*
⁶Man is a mere phantom as he goes to and fro:
  He bustles about, but only in vain;
  he heaps up wealth, not knowing who will get it.

⁷But now, Lord, what do I look for?
  My hope is in you.
⁸Save me from all my transgressions;
  do not make me the scorn of fools.
⁹I was silent; I would not open my mouth,
  for you are the one who has done this.
¹⁰Remove your scourge from me;
  I am overcome by the blow of your hand.
¹¹You rebuke and discipline men for their sin;
  you consume their wealth like a moth—
  each man is but a breath. . . .   *Selah*

¹³Look away from me, that I may rejoice again
  before I depart and am no more."

When We Speak Foolishly

When former law professor Phillip E. Johnson had a stroke, he was so afraid of being mentally and physically impaired that he wished the doctor would give him a painless death. He said, "That was a foolish thought, of course, but not the last foolish thought I was to have."

In my own pastoral ministry, I've heard some of God's children express thoughts worse than Johnson's—even rebellious words against God.

Psalm 39 offers comfort to people who regret the thoughtless things they've said in times of despair. David was gravely ill and desperate when he wrote the psalm. At first he kept silent lest he speak foolishly (vv. 1–3). But when he could contain himself no longer, he prayed a wonderful prayer (vv. 4–9).

But in verses 10 and 11 his tone began to change. According to the British scholar Derek Kidner, David spoke foolishly when he said, "Look away from me . . . before I depart and am no more" (v. 13). David expressed a hopeless attitude toward death and said to God, in effect, "Leave me alone." Kidner comments that God included this prayer in the Bible to reassure us that when we say things out of desperation He understands. And when we tell Him how sorry we are, He graciously forgives.

—*Herb VanderLugt*

Psalm 40:1–10

¹ I waited patiently for the LORD;
    he turned to me and heard my cry.
² He lifted me out of the slimy pit,
    out of the mud and mire;
  he set my feet on a rock
    and gave me a firm place to stand.
³ He put a new song in my mouth,
    a hymn of praise to our God.
  Many will see and fear
    and put their trust in the LORD.

⁴ Blessed is the man
    who makes the LORD his trust,
  who does not look to the proud,
    to those who turn aside to false gods.
⁵ Many, O LORD my God,
    are the wonders you have done.
  The things you planned for us
    no one can recount to you;
  were I to speak and tell of them,
    they would be too many to declare.

⁶ Sacrifice and offering you did not desire,
    but my ears you have pierced;
  burnt offerings and sin offerings
    you did not require.
⁷ Then I said, "Here I am, I have come—
    it is written about me in the scroll.
⁸ I desire to do your will, O my God;
    your law is within my heart."

⁹ I proclaim righteousness in the great assembly;
    I do not seal my lips,
    as you know, O LORD.
¹⁰ I do not hide your righteousness in my heart;
    I speak of your faithfulness and salvation.
  I do not conceal your love and your truth
    from the great assembly.

New Songs

The song of the humpback whale is one of the strangest in nature. It is a weird combination of high- and low-pitched groaning. Those who have studied the humpback whale say their songs are noteworthy because these giants of the deep are continually changing them. New patterns are added and old ones eliminated so that over a period of time the whale actually sings a whole new song.

There's a sense in which a Christian should be continually composing new songs of praise around the fresh mercies of God. Unfortunately, many of us just keep singing "the same old song."

We must repeatedly affirm the fundamentals of our faith. But as the psalmist tells us, the works of God's deliverance in the lives of His people are many. His works, which are more than we can count, give us reasons to express our praise to Him in numerous ways (Psalm 40:5).

So why do we express our testimony of God's saving grace in the same old way year after year? A fresh experience of the mercies of the cross and of Christ's resurrection power should continually fill our hearts and minds with new songs.

The gospel story never changes—thank God for that. But our songs of praise should be ever new.

—Mart DeHaan

Psalm 41

¹ Blessed is he who considers the poor;
　　The LORD will deliver him in time of trouble.
² The LORD will preserve him and keep him alive,
　　And he will be blessed on the earth;
　　You will not deliver him to the will of his enemies.
³ The LORD will strengthen him on his bed of illness;
　　You will sustain him on his sickbed.

⁴ I said, "LORD, be merciful to me;
　　Heal my soul, for I have sinned against You."
⁵ My enemies speak evil of me:
　　"When will he die, and his name perish?"
⁶ And if he comes to see me, he speaks lies;
　　His heart gathers iniquity to itself;
　　When he goes out, he tells it.

⁷ All who hate me whisper together against me;
　　Against me they devise my hurt.
⁸ "An evil disease," they say, "clings to him.
　　And now that he lies down, he will rise up no more."
⁹ Even my own familiar friend in whom I trusted,
　　Who ate my bread,
　　Has lifted up his heel against me.

¹⁰ But You, O LORD, be merciful to me, and raise me up,
　　That I may repay them.
¹¹ By this I know that You are well pleased with me,
　　Because my enemy does not triumph over me.
¹² As for me, You uphold me in my integrity,
　　And set me before Your face forever.

¹³ Blessed be the LORD God of Israel
　　From everlasting to everlasting!
　　Amen and Amen.

(NKJV)

Consider the Poor

You may have heard of the blessings Jesus spoke of in His Sermon on the Mount (Matthew 5:1–10). Here's a "blessing" from the Old Testament that is less well-known: "Blessed is he who considers the poor" (Psalm 41:1).

The Hebrew word translated *considers* means "to take thought for others." The word translated *poor* means "those in need."

There are many people around us who are poor—in love, in hope, and in the knowledge of God. Even though we cannot solve all their problems, we can show them that we care.

We may not have lots of money, but we can give of ourselves. We can let needy people know that we're thinking of them. We can listen as they tell their stories. We can treat them with courtesy and respect. We can pray for them. We can write letters of encouragement. We can tell them about Jesus. If we can do nothing else, we can love them.

Think about those who live only for themselves, always trying to get ahead, looking for the next thing to make them happy. Compare them with people who give themselves to others. Which ones possess inner calm, strength, and joy?

The place of God's blessing is easily entered: Consider the poor.

—*David Roper*

Psalm 42:5–11

⁵Why are you downcast, O my soul?
    Why so disturbed within me?
Put your hope in God,
    for I will yet praise him,
    my Savior and ⁶ my God.

My soul is downcast within me;
    therefore I will remember you
from the land of the Jordan,
    the heights of Hermon—from Mount Mizar.
⁷Deep calls to deep
    in the roar of your waterfalls;
all your waves and breakers
    have swept over me.

⁸By day the LORD directs his love,
    at night his song is with me—
    a prayer to the God of my life.

⁹I say to God my Rock,
    "Why have you forgotten me?
Why must I go about mourning,
    oppressed by the enemy?"
¹⁰My bones suffer mortal agony
    as my foes taunt me,
saying to me all day long,
    "Where is your God?"

¹¹Why are you downcast, O my soul?
    Why so disturbed within me?
Put your hope in God,
    for I will yet praise him,
    my Savior and my God.

Night

In his riveting and unsettling book *Night*, Elie Weisel describes his boyhood experiences as one of the countless victims of the Holocaust. Ripped from his home and separated from everyone in his family except his father (who would die in the death camps), Weisel suffered a dark night of the soul such as few will experience. It challenged his views and beliefs about God. His innocence and faith became sacrifices on the altar of man's evil and sin's darkness.

David experienced his own dark night of the soul, which many scholars believe motivated his writing of Psalm 42. Harried and hounded, probably as he was pursued by his rebellious son Absalom (2 Samuel 16–18), David echoed the pain and fear that can be felt in the isolation of night. It's the place where darkness grips us and forces us to consider the anguish of our heart and ask hard questions of God. The psalmist lamented God's seeming absence, yet in it all he found a night song (v. 8) that gave him peace and confidence for the difficulties ahead.

When we struggle in the night, we can be confident that God is at work in the darkness. We can say with the psalmist, "Hope in God, for I will yet praise him, my Savior and my God" (v. 11).

—*Bill Crowder*

Psalm 46

¹God is our refuge and strength,
 an ever-present help in trouble.
²Therefore we will not fear, though the earth give way
 and the mountains fall into the heart of the sea,
³though its waters roar and foam
 and the mountains quake with their surging.   *Selah*

⁴There is a river whose streams make glad the city of God,
 the holy place where the Most High dwells.
⁵God is within her, she will not fall;
 God will help her at break of day.
⁶Nations are in uproar, kingdoms fall;
 he lifts his voice, the earth melts.

⁷The LORD Almighty is with us;
 the God of Jacob is our fortress.   *Selah*

⁸Come and see the works of the LORD,
 the desolations he has brought on the earth.
⁹He makes wars cease to the ends of the earth;
 he breaks the bow and shatters the spear,
 he burns the shields with fire.
¹⁰"Be still, and know that I am God;
 I will be exalted among the nations,
 I will be exalted in the earth."

¹¹The LORD Almighty is with us;
 the God of Jacob is our fortress.   *Selah*

Help!

People are supposed to call 911 for emergencies only, but many people don't understand or follow the rule. Police emergency operators in Colorado Springs have received calls from people reporting a TV set that wasn't working, asking when it was going to stop snowing, and wanting to report an identification theft while they remained anonymous.

I have often wondered if many of our prayers for help sound frivolous to God. It's impossible to know, but there's one thing we can be assured of: In our times of need, the Lord not only hears our cries, He is present with us.

Psalm 46 describes times of great calamity, including war and natural disasters. Yet it is a song of trust that begins and ends with the same affirmation: "God is our refuge and strength, an ever-present help in trouble . . . The Lord Almighty is with us; the God of Jacob is our fortress" (vv. 1, 11).

The Lord is always at work accomplishing His purposes—even when the world seems to be falling apart. He tells us, "Be still, and know that I am God; I will be exalted among the nations, I will be exalted in the earth!" (v. 10).

We don't have to fear. When we call for help, we know that He hears and will come near.

—*David McCasland*

Psalm 47

¹Clap your hands, all you nations;
    shout to God with cries of joy.
²How awesome is the LORD Most High,
    the great King over all the earth!
³He subdued nations under us,
    peoples under our feet.
⁴He chose our inheritance for us,
    the pride of Jacob, whom he loved.   *Selah*

⁵God has ascended amid shouts of joy,
    the LORD amid the sounding of trumpets.
⁶Sing praises to God, sing praises;
    sing praises to our King, sing praises.
⁷For God is the King of all the earth;
    sing to him a psalm of praise.

⁸God reigns over the nations;
    God is seated on his holy throne.
⁹The nobles of the nations assemble
    as the people of the God of Abraham,
for the kings of the earth belong to God;
    he is greatly exalted.

Awesome!

It's an often-used word, and we hear it in the most unusual contexts. It's the word *awesome*.

My nine-year-old grandson Josh and I were playing with a radio-controlled racecar set on the living room floor. Several times he would say, "Awesome!"

On another occasion, as my wife and I were leaving a restaurant, the manager, who was standing by the door, asked, "How was everything, folks?" "Fine," I replied. "Awesome!" he said.

These two occasions set me to thinking: While it's fun to play with my grandson and to enjoy a meal at a restaurant, are these experiences really awesome? So I consulted Mr. Webster's unabridged dictionary. The primary definition lists *awesome* as "deeply reverent," "dreadful," "awful." I remembered the time that I stood on the south rim of the Grand Canyon. That was truly an awesome experience.

Then I thought of a more awe-inspiring reality still. It's knowing the Creator and Sustainer of the entire universe. No wonder the psalmist wrote, "How awesome is the LORD Most High" (Psalm 47:2).

The next time we hear the word *awesome*, may it remind us of our great God, who truly is *awesome*!

—*Dennis DeHaan*

Psalm 51:1–13

[1] Have mercy on me, O God,
  according to your unfailing love;
 according to your great compassion
  blot out my transgressions.
[2] Wash away all my iniquity
  and cleanse me from my sin.

[3] For I know my transgressions,
  and my sin is always before me.
[4] Against you, you only, have I sinned
  and done what is evil in your sight,
 so that you are proved right when you speak
  and justified when you judge.
[5] Surely I was sinful at birth,
  sinful from the time my mother conceived me.
[6] Surely you desire truth in the inner parts;
  you teach me wisdom in the inmost place.

[7] Cleanse me with hyssop, and I will be clean;
  wash me, and I will be whiter than snow.
[8] Let me hear joy and gladness;
  let the bones you have crushed rejoice.
[9] Hide your face from my sins
  and blot out all my iniquity.

[10] Create in me a pure heart, O God,
  and renew a steadfast spirit within me.
[11] Do not cast me from your presence
  or take your Holy Spirit from me.
[12] Restore to me the joy of your salvation
  and grant me a willing spirit, to sustain me.

[13] Then I will teach transgressors your ways,
  and sinners will turn back to you.

Repenting and Rejoicing

A Christian woman asked another believer how he was doing. With a broad smile he replied, "Repenting and rejoicing, sister!"

I believe this man was walking in a spirit of repentance—daily confessing and turning from sins and rejoicing in God's forgiveness.

Because honest repentance involves sorrow, we may forget that repenting leads to rejoicing. When we first repent and become new believers, we experience great joy. But if we then choose to live with unconfessed sin, our joy is lost.

David believed his joy could be restored. After pouring out his prayer of repentance to God, he made this humble plea: "Restore to me the joy of your salvation" (Psalm 51:12). As David turned back to the Lord, his sense of purpose returned: "Then I will teach transgressors your ways, and sinners will turn back to you" (v. 13). Through his faith in a forgiving and merciful God, David began rejoicing again in his salvation (vv. 14–15).

Do you sometimes lose the joy of your salvation because you fail to deal with your sins? If you'll confess them, God will forgive you (1 John 1:9). He'll restore your joy and help you overcome sins that trouble you. That's what it means to be a "repenting and rejoicing" Christian.

—Joanie Yoder

Psalm 54

[1] Save me, O God, by your name;
    vindicate me by your might.
[2] Hear my prayer, O God;
    listen to the words of my mouth.

[3] Strangers are attacking me;
    ruthless men seek my life—
    men without regard for God.   *Selah*

[4] Surely God is my help;
    the Lord is the one who sustains me.

[5] Let evil recoil on those who slander me;
    in your faithfulness destroy them.

[6] I will sacrifice a freewill offering to you;
    I will praise your name, O LORD,
    for it is good.
[7] For he has delivered me from all my troubles,
    and my eyes have looked in triumph on my foes.

Get Up!

I hadn't been water-skiing in fifteen years, but when friends offered to take my son-in-law Todd and me out on the lake last summer, how could I say no? It seemed like a good idea until I watched Todd have trouble getting upright on his skis. He had done a lot of skiing, but as he tried to get up on one ski, he kept falling. So when it came to my turn, I didn't have a lot of confidence.

Fortunately, my friend who is a competitive skier stayed with me in the water and coached me about what to do. She said, "Let the boat pull you up," and "Be strong!" These seemingly contradictory statements made all the difference. I did both—I trusted the boat to do its job, and I hung on with all my strength. The first time the boat took off, I got up and enjoyed a great ride around the lake.

When life has you down—whether through sorrow that seems too hard to bear or circumstances that make each day a morning-to-night grind—my friend's advice can help. First, let God pull you up by His power (Psalm 54:1–4). Then, hold on to His hand. Cling to Him and "be strong in the Lord and in his mighty power" (Ephesians 6:10).

Trust His power and hold on. He will give you the strength to keep from falling (Isaiah 40:31).

—Dave Branon

Psalm 55:16–23

¹⁶But I call to God,
    and the LORD saves me.
¹⁷Evening, morning and noon
    I cry out in distress,
    and he hears my voice.
¹⁸He ransoms me unharmed
    from the battle waged against me,
    even though many oppose me.
¹⁹God, who is enthroned forever,
    will hear them and afflict them—   *Selah*
men who never change their ways
    and have no fear of God.

²⁰My companion attacks his friends;
    he violates his covenant.
²¹His speech is smooth as butter,
    yet war is in his heart;
his words are more soothing than oil,
    yet they are drawn swords.

²²Cast your cares on the LORD
    and he will sustain you;
    he will never let the righteous fall.
²³But you, O God, will bring down the wicked
    into the pit of corruption;
bloodthirsty and deceitful men
    will not live out half their days.

But as for me, I trust in you.

Morning, Noon, and Night

In May 2003, a powerful earthquake struck northern Algeria. TV news images showed distraught people searching the rubble for survivors, while others numbly visited hospitals and morgues to see if their loved ones were alive or dead. Families stood together weeping and crying out for help. Their burden of uncertainty and grief could be seen, heard, and felt.

If you've experienced an intense feeling of loss, you'll appreciate the words of David in Psalm 55, penned during a painful time in his life. Oppressed by the wicked, hated by his enemies, and betrayed by a friend, David spoke of the anxiety and anguish that threatened to crush his spirit: "Fear and trembling have beset me; horror has overwhelmed me" (v. 5).

But instead of caving in to fear, David poured out his heart to God: "But I call to God, and the LORD saves me. Evening, morning and noon I cry out in distress, and he hears my voice" (vv. 16–17).

Prayer lifts our eyes from personal tragedy to the compassion of God. It enables us to cast our burdens on the Lord instead of breaking under their weight. When our hearts are filled with pain, it's good to call on God in prayer—morning, noon, and night.

—David McCasland

Psalm 56

¹Be merciful to me, O God, for men hotly pursue me;
    all day long they press their attack.
²My slanderers pursue me all day long;
    many are attacking me in their pride.

³When I am afraid,
    I will trust in you.
⁴In God, whose word I praise,
    in God I trust; I will not be afraid.
    What can mortal man do to me?

⁵All day long they twist my words;
    they are always plotting to harm me.
⁶They conspire, they lurk,
    they watch my steps,
    eager to take my life.

⁷On no account let them escape;
    in your anger, O God, bring down the nations.
⁸Record my lament;
    list my tears on your scroll—
    are they not in your record?

⁹Then my enemies will turn back
    when I call for help.
    By this I will know that God is for me.
¹⁰In God, whose word I praise,
    in the LORD, whose word I praise—
¹¹in God I trust; I will not be afraid.
    What can man do to me?

¹²I am under vows to you, O God;
    I will present my thank offerings to you.
¹³For you have delivered me from death
    and my feet from stumbling,
that I may walk before God
    in the light of life.

Life Is Real

In the comic strip *Peanuts*, Lucy had just broken the news to Linus that children cannot live at home forever. Eventually they grow up and move away. Then she said that when he left she would get his room. But Linus quickly reminded her that at some time she too would have to leave home. When this realization hit Lucy, she was shocked, but she quickly came up with a solution. She turned the TV up loud, crawled into her beanbag chair with a bowl of ice cream, and refused to think about it.

Avoiding unpleasant circumstances is not as easy as Lucy thinks. Life's realities cannot be avoided. We may try to run and hide, but struggles and trials have a way of dogging our footsteps and eventually catching up with us.

Instead, we should face up to our problems. The psalmist David did this when beset by persistent foes and false friends. He didn't try to minimize his danger; he acknowledged the storm that was raging around him and looked to the Lord. He wrote, "In God I trust; I will not be afraid" (Psalm 56:4).

Let's follow David's example—not Lucy's. Facing up to life's difficulties may be a frightening experience. But when we trust God and draw close to Him, we'll experience real deliverance.

—*Paul Van Gorder*

Psalm 57

¹Have mercy on me, O God, have mercy on me,
  for in you my soul takes refuge.
 I will take refuge in the shadow of your wings
  until the disaster has passed.

²I cry out to God Most High,
  to God, who fulfills his purpose for me.
³He sends from heaven and saves me,
  rebuking those who hotly pursue me;   *Selah*
 God sends his love and his faithfulness.

⁴I am in the midst of lions;
  I lie among ravenous beasts—
 men whose teeth are spears and arrows,
  whose tongues are sharp swords.

⁵Be exalted, O God, above the heavens;
  let your glory be over all the earth.

⁶They spread a net for my feet—
  I was bowed down in distress.
 They dug a pit in my path—
  but they have fallen into it themselves.   *Selah*

⁷My heart is steadfast, O God,
  my heart is steadfast;
  I will sing and make music.
⁸Awake, my soul!
  Awake, harp and lyre!
  I will awaken the dawn.

⁹I will praise you, O Lord, among the nations;
  I will sing of you among the peoples.
¹⁰For great is your love, reaching to the heavens;
  your faithfulness reaches to the skies.

¹¹Be exalted, O God, above the heavens;
  let your glory be over all the earth.

Our Place of Refuge

It is believed that David wrote Psalm 57 while fleeing from King Saul, who had hatred in his heart for the former shepherd boy. David ducked into a cave and barely escaped his pursuer. He was safe temporarily, but the threat was still there.

We've all been there. Maybe not in a cave, but pursued by something that strikes fear into our hearts. Perhaps it is the deep sorrow that follows the death of someone we love. Maybe it's the fear of an unknown future. Or it could be an oppressive physical illness that won't go away.

In such circumstances, God does not always remove the difficulty, but He is present to help us. We wish that He would swoop in and whisk us to safety—just as David may have wished for a quick end to Saul's pursuit. We plead with God to stop the pain and make the road to tomorrow smooth and straight. We beg Him to eliminate our struggle. But the difficulty remains. It is then that we have to take refuge in God as David did. While hiding in that cave, he said, "I will take refuge in the shadow of your wings until the disaster has passed" (Psalm 57:1).

Are you in the middle of trouble? Take refuge in the Most High God.

—*Dave Branon*

Psalm 59:9–17

⁹O my Strength, I watch for you;
  you, O God, are my fortress, ¹⁰ my loving God.

  God will go before me
    and will let me gloat over those who slander me.
¹¹But do not kill them, O Lord our shield,
    or my people will forget.
  In your might make them wander about,
    and bring them down.
¹²For the sins of their mouths,
    for the words of their lips,
    let them be caught in their pride.
  For the curses and lies they utter,
¹³consume them in wrath,
    consume them till they are no more.
  Then it will be known to the ends of the earth
    that God rules over Jacob.   *Selah*

¹⁴They return at evening,
    snarling like dogs,
    and prowl about the city.
¹⁵They wander about for food
    and howl if not satisfied.
¹⁶But I will sing of your strength,
    in the morning I will sing of your love;
for you are my fortress,
    my refuge in times of trouble.

¹⁷O my Strength, I sing praise to you;
    you, O God, are my fortress, my loving God.

Finding Security

After a man shot and killed two people at Los Angeles International Airport in 2002, some began insisting that armed guards be placed at every check-in area. Others said that individuals should be screened before entering an airport terminal. But a consultant on airport security said, "If you move the checkpoint, all you're going to do is push the problem to another part of the airport. There will always be a public area that is vulnerable to these kinds of attacks."

In a world where violence and terrorism may strike anytime, anyplace, where can we find security? Where can we be safe?

The Bible says that our security is not in human protection but in God himself. The book of Psalms contains more than forty references to taking refuge in the Lord, many of them from David's experience of being pursued by his enemies. In his prayers for help, he centered his hope in the Lord: "You are my fortress, my refuge in times of trouble. O my Strength, I sing praise to you; you, O God, are my fortress, my loving God" (Psalm 59:16–17).

God doesn't guarantee to protect us from difficulty and physical harm, but He does promise to be our refuge in every situation. In Him we find real security.

—David McCasland

Psalm 62:1–8

[1] Truly my soul silently waits for God;
   From Him comes my salvation.
[2] He only is my rock and my salvation;
   He is my defense;
   I shall not be greatly moved.

[3] How long will you attack a man?
   You shall be slain, all of you,
   Like a leaning wall and a tottering fence.
[4] They only consult to cast him down from his high position;
   They delight in lies;
   They bless with their mouth,
   But they curse inwardly.   *Selah*

[5] My soul, wait silently for God alone,
   For my expectation is from Him.
[6] He only is my rock and my salvation;
   He is my defense;
   I shall not be moved.
[7] In God is my salvation and my glory;
   The rock of my strength,
   And my refuge, is in God.

[8] Trust in Him at all times, you people;
   Pour out your heart before Him;
   God is a refuge for us.   *Selah*

(NKJV)

The Beauty of Silence

Written on the wall behind the pulpit of the church we attended in my teens were these words: "The Lord is in His holy temple. Let all the earth keep silence before Him" (Habakkuk 2:20). And keep silence we did! All eight of us boys said nothing to one another as we sat waiting for the service to begin.

I loved this quiet time and often succeeded in pushing thoughts about girls and the Detroit Tigers out of my mind. The best I could, I tried to reflect on the wonder of God and His salvation. And in the silence I often sensed His presence.

Today we live in a noisy world. Many people can't even drive without music blaring from their car or the beat of the bass vibrating their vehicle. Even many church services are marked more by noise than by quiet reflection.

In ancient times the pagans cried out in a noisy frenzy to their idols (1 Kings 18:25–29). In sharp contrast, the psalmist saw the wisdom of silence, because in quiet reverence God can be heard. In the stillness of the night under a starry sky, in a hushed sanctuary, or in a quiet room at home, we can meet the living God and hear Him speak.

The psalmist's words are relevant today: "Wait silently for God alone" (Psalm 62:5).

—*Herb VanderLugt*

Psalm 63

[1] O God, you are my God,
    earnestly I seek you;
my soul thirsts for you,
    my body longs for you,
in a dry and weary land
    where there is no water.

[2] I have seen you in the sanctuary
    and beheld your power and your glory.
[3] Because your love is better than life,
    my lips will glorify you.
[4] I will praise you as long as I live,
    and in your name I will lift up my hands.
[5] My soul will be satisfied as with the richest of foods;
    with singing lips my mouth will praise you.

[6] On my bed I remember you;
    I think of you through the watches of the night.
[7] Because you are my help,
    I sing in the shadow of your wings.
[8] My soul clings to you;
    your right hand upholds me.

[9] They who seek my life will be destroyed;
    they will go down to the depths of the earth.
[10] They will be given over to the sword
    and become food for jackals.

[11] But the king will rejoice in God;
    all who swear by God's name will praise him,
    while the mouths of liars will be silenced.

Ignoring God

As a former high school teacher and occasional college instructor, I had this recurring thought: How terrible it would be to stand up in front of a classroom of students and have no one pay attention—to talk and have no one listen, to give instructions and have the students ignore them.

None of us enjoys being ignored. If we're in a conversation with a friend, it hurts to have our words disregarded. If we're in a store looking for help, it's irritating to be ignored by the clerks. When we're struggling with a problem, it's painful when no one offers to help.

Imagine, then, how it must grieve God when we ignore Him. Think of how His heart of love must break when, despite the fact that He dwells within us through the Holy Spirit, we act as if He's not there. Or consider how He must feel when His guidelines contained in the book He gave us are ignored.

Let's be careful not to ignore God. In ways large and small, let's keep Him in our thoughts moment by moment. We do that by reading the inspired writings He has given us; by spending time in prayer and listening for His still, small voice; by thinking about His presence; by serving others in His name. May we be able to say with the psalmist, "My soul clings to you" (Psalm 63:8).

—*Dave Branon*

Psalm 65:1–8

[1] Praise awaits you, O God, in Zion;
    to you our vows will be fulfilled.
[2] O you who hear prayer,
    to you all men will come.
[3] When we were overwhelmed by sins,
    you forgave our transgressions.
[4] Blessed are those you choose
    and bring near to live in your courts!
 We are filled with the good things of your house,
    of your holy temple.

[5] You answer us with awesome deeds of righteousness,
    O God our Savior,
 the hope of all the ends of the earth
    and of the farthest seas,
[6] who formed the mountains by your power,
    having armed yourself with strength,
[7] who stilled the roaring of the seas,
    the roaring of their waves,
    and the turmoil of the nations.
[8] Those living far away fear your wonders;
    where morning dawns and evening fades
    you call forth songs of joy.

Letters to God

Every year thousands of letters addressed to God find their way to a post office in Jerusalem. One letter, addressed to "God of Israel," was from a person who requested assistance in getting a job as a bulldozer driver. Another said: "Please help me to be happy, to find a nice job and a good wife—soon." One man asked forgiveness for stealing money from a grocery store when he was a child.

But were those heartfelt requests heard by God? The psalmist said that God is the one who hears prayer (Psalm 65:2). Whether we say our prayers silently, voice them aloud, or write them on paper, they go directly to God. But He does not answer every request as we would wish. Our petitions may be self-serving (James 4:3), or sin may be blocking our fellowship with Him (Psalm 66:18).

More than giving us what we want, the Lord knows our deepest needs, and He wants us to discover the joy of His presence each day. Because of our faith in Christ, praying becomes our means of communion with God, not just a list of things we want from Him.

In His wisdom, God hears all our prayers. In His grace, He offers forgiveness for all our sins. In His love, He gives us eternal and abundant life through His Son.

—*David McCasland*

Psalm 66:1–12

[1] Shout with joy to God, all the earth!
[2] Sing the glory of his name;
    make his praise glorious!
[3] Say to God, "How awesome are your deeds!
    So great is your power
    that your enemies cringe before you.
[4] All the earth bows down to you;
    they sing praise to you,
    they sing praise to your name."   *Selah*

[5] Come and see what God has done,
    how awesome his works in man's behalf!
[6] He turned the sea into dry land,
    they passed through the waters on foot—
    come, let us rejoice in him.
[7] He rules forever by his power,
    his eyes watch the nations—
    let not the rebellious rise up against him.   *Selah*

[8] Praise our God, O peoples,
    let the sound of his praise be heard;
[9] he has preserved our lives
    and kept our feet from slipping.
[10] For you, O God, tested us;
    you refined us like silver.
[11] You brought us into prison
    and laid burdens on our backs.
[12] You let men ride over our heads;
    we went through fire and water,
    but you brought us to a place of abundance.

Tried by Fire

"The main end of life is not to do but to become," F. B. Meyer said. And for this we are being prepared every day. As silver is refined by fire, the heart is often refined in the furnace of sadness. The psalmist said in his sorrow, "We went through fire" (Psalm 66:12).

The refining process may be very painful, but it will not destroy us, for the Refiner sits by the furnace tending the flame. He will not allow us to be tried beyond our endurance; it is for our good.

We may not understand why we have to endure such misery year after year. The ordeal seems endless and pointless. Our days are wasted, or so it appears. We feel as if we are doing nothing of lasting significance.

But God is doing what matters—we are being refined. He is placing us into a crucible in which we acquire patience, meekness, humility, compassion, and the other "quiet" virtues our souls naturally lack.

So don't be afraid and don't fret. Your present trial, as painful as it may be, has been screened through God's wisdom and love. The Refiner sits beside the crucible tempering the flames, monitoring the process, waiting patiently until His face is mirrored in the surface.

—*David Roper*

Psalm 69:29–36

²⁹ I am in pain and distress;
    may your salvation, O God, protect me.

³⁰ I will praise God's name in song
    and glorify him with thanksgiving.
³¹ This will please the LORD more than an ox,
    more than a bull with its horns and hoofs.
³² The poor will see and be glad—
    you who seek God, may your hearts live!
³³ The LORD hears the needy
    and does not despise his captive people.

³⁴ Let heaven and earth praise him,
    the seas and all that move in them,
³⁵ for God will save Zion
    and rebuild the cities of Judah.
  Then people will settle there and possess it;
³⁶ the children of his servants will inherit it,
    and those who love his name will dwell there.

Be Glad!

For several days after my husband and his brother sang a duet in church of "Be Ye Glad," I was unable to get the lyrics by Michael Blanchard out of my mind. But they're good words to get stuck on, reminding us to be glad because the Lord's grace has paid our debts in full.

Ancient Israel's beloved songwriter and king often wrote about gladness. In three consecutive songs, David spoke of being glad: Psalm 68:3; 69:32; 70:4. His lyrics assure us that it's not the rich or the powerful that have reason to be glad but those who are poor or humble and right with God.

David expanded on this theme in another song: "Blessed is he whose transgressions are forgiven, whose sins are covered . . . Rejoice in the LORD and be glad, you righteous; sing, all you who are upright in heart!" (Psalm 32:1, 11).

If you are feeling poor and powerless today, you can still be glad. You can have something of far more value: a debt-free relationship with God.

When we stop defending our own sinful ways and humbly acknowledge that God's ways are right, true gladness will spring forth in songs of glorious praise.

—Julie Ackerman Link

Psalm 71:1–14

[1] In you, O LORD, I have taken refuge;
    let me never be put to shame.
[2] Rescue me and deliver me in your righteousness;
    turn your ear to me and save me.
[3] Be my rock of refuge,
    to which I can always go;
    give the command to save me,
    for you are my rock and my fortress.
[4] Deliver me, O my God, from the hand of the wicked,
    from the grasp of evil and cruel men.

[5] For you have been my hope, O Sovereign LORD,
    my confidence since my youth.
[6] From birth I have relied on you;
    you brought me forth from my mother's womb.
    I will ever praise you.
[7] I have become like a portent to many,
    but you are my strong refuge.
[8] My mouth is filled with your praise,
    declaring your splendor all day long.

[9] Do not cast me away when I am old;
    do not forsake me when my strength is gone.
[10] For my enemies speak against me;
    those who wait to kill me conspire together.
[11] They say, "God has forsaken him;
    pursue him and seize him,
    for no one will rescue him."
[12] Be not far from me, O God;
    come quickly, O my God, to help me.
[13] May my accusers perish in shame;
    may those who want to harm me
    be covered with scorn and disgrace.

[14] But as for me, I will always have hope;
    I will praise you more and more.

Life's Seasons

When we are young, we can't wait to grow up. When we are old, we look back longingly to former years. But God intends that we joyfully take each season of life as it comes. Whatever our age, He imparts what we need to be all that we can be. He asks us to commit our way to Him and accept the struggles He allows and the strength He provides.

A woman who was facing the difficulties of aging asked Bible teacher J. Robertson McQuilkin, "Why does God let us get old and weak?" McQuilkin replied, "I think God has planned the strength and beauty of youth to be physical. But the strength and beauty of old age is spiritual. We gradually lose the strength and beauty that is temporary so we'll be sure to concentrate on the strength and beauty that is forever. And so we'll be eager to leave the temporary, deteriorating part of us and be truly homesick for our eternal home. If we stayed young and strong and beautiful, we might never want to leave."

Are you in life's springtime? Trust God's timing to fulfill your dreams. Are you in life's summer or autumn? Face your daily challenges head-on. And if you feel winter's chill, draw close to the Lord. His presence can make every season of life one of strength and beauty.

—*Dennis DeHaan*

Psalm 73:21–28

21 When my heart was grieved
  and my spirit embittered,
22 I was senseless and ignorant;
  I was a brute beast before you.

23 Yet I am always with you;
  you hold me by my right hand.
24 You guide me with your counsel,
  and afterward you will take me into glory.
25 Whom have I in heaven but you?
  And earth has nothing I desire besides you.
26 My flesh and my heart may fail,
  but God is the strength of my heart
  and my portion forever.

27 Those who are far from you will perish;
  you destroy all who are unfaithful to you.
28 But as for me, it is good to be near God.
  I have made the Sovereign LORD my refuge;
  I will tell of all your deeds.

Got Thirst?

Health experts tell us we should drink at least sixty-four ounces of water each day. It may reduce the risk of heart attack, give our skin a healthy glow, and help us lose weight. We should drink even more water during exercise or if we live in a hot or dry climate. Even if we're not thirsty, we ought to drink water anyway.

Our thirst for God is even more beneficial. When we're spiritually dry, we long to hear from Him through His Word, and we search for even a drop of knowledge about Him. When we're exercising our faith in a new way, we want to be close to Him and receive His strength. Our thirst for God may increase when we see the sinfulness of people around us or when we gain a new awareness of our own sin and need for Him.

Spiritual thirst is a metaphor used throughout Scripture. Asaph thirsted for answers in his questioning psalm. When he saw the wicked prospering, he cried out to God to understand why (Psalm 73:16). He found the Lord to be his strength and realized that he desired nothing but Him (vv. 25–26).

If we're spiritually thirsty, we can follow Asaph's example and draw near to God (v. 28). He will satisfy us, yet give us a deeper thirst for himself. We'll learn to desire Him above all else.

—*Anne Cetas*

Psalm 77:7–15

7 "Will the Lord reject forever?
    Will he never show his favor again?
8 Has his unfailing love vanished forever?
    Has his promise failed for all time?
9 Has God forgotten to be merciful?
    Has he in anger withheld his compassion?"   *Selah*

10 Then I thought, "To this I will appeal:
    the years of the right hand of the Most High."
11 I will remember the deeds of the LORD;
    yes, I will remember your miracles of long ago.
12 I will meditate on all your works
    and consider all your mighty deeds.

13 Your ways, O God, are holy.
    What god is so great as our God?
14 You are the God who performs miracles;
    you display your power among the peoples.
15 With your mighty arm you redeemed your people,
    the descendants of Jacob and Joseph.   *Selah*

Days of Doubt

In 1970, Ronald Dunn began keeping a record of answered prayers and special blessings in a little book. He misplaced the book but found it again several years later at a time when his faith was floundering. He was surprised that he had forgotten most of the incidents he had written about.

As he was reading, something happened. "My memory of God's faithfulness was revived and my sagging faith began to recover," he said. "Remembering had restored my confidence in the Lord." Dunn now encourages Christians to keep a book of remembrance, recording God's activity in their lives. "One day," he writes, "it may mean the difference between victory and defeat."

In Psalm 77, Asaph's faith was also floundering. After listing his serious doubts, he asked, "Has God forgotten to be merciful?" (v. 9). Suddenly he stopped and said, "To this I will appeal: the years of the right hand of the Most High. I will remember the deeds of the LORD; yes, I will remember your miracles of long ago" (vv. 10–11). The act of remembering obviously revived his faith. Just read the rest of the psalm!

Why not create your own book of remembrance, recording God's wonderful deeds? Then read it often, especially on days of doubt.

—*Joanie Yoder*

[49] He unleashed against them his hot anger,
his wrath, indignation and hostility—
a band of destroying angels.
[50] He prepared a path for his anger;
he did not spare them from death
but gave them over to the plague.
[51] He struck down all the firstborn of Egypt,
the firstfruits of manhood in the tents of Ham.
[52] But he brought his people out like a flock;
he led them like sheep through the desert.
[53] He guided them safely, so they were unafraid;
but the sea engulfed their enemies.
[54] Thus he brought them to the border of his holy land,
to the hill country his right hand had taken.
[55] He drove out nations before them
and allotted their lands to them as an inheritance;
he settled the tribes of Israel in their homes.

His Highest Blessing

When John Henry Jowett was a young man, he was so intent on pursuing a law career that he didn't ask the Lord what He wanted him to do with his life. One day he met his old Sunday school teacher, who asked him what he was going to do with his many talents. Jowett replied that he was studying to be a lawyer. Disappointed, his friend said, "I've prayed for years that you would go into the ministry."

This startled the brilliant young student and set him to thinking seriously about entering the ministry. Later Jowett wrote, "I then sought God's will and reverently obeyed His call. Now, after thirty-five years in His service, I can say I've never regretted my choice."

Instead of charting your own future, seek God's direction. Because His will is based on His infinite love and wisdom, you may be sure that your highest joy and greatest fulfillment will be found in doing what He wants you to do.

God doesn't call everyone to be a minister or a missionary, but He will guide you into the place of His special choosing if you surrender to Him. He always leads to the calling of greatest usefulness.

When you follow the Lord, life becomes a beautiful adventure. He'll always direct your steps along the paths of His highest blessing.

—Henry Bosch

Psalm 81:8–16

[8] "Hear, O my people, and I will warn you—
   if you would but listen to me, O Israel!
[9] You shall have no foreign god among you;
   you shall not bow down to an alien god.
[10] I am the LORD your God,
   who brought you up out of Egypt.
   Open wide your mouth and I will fill it.

[11] "But my people would not listen to me;
   Israel would not submit to me.
[12] So I gave them over to their stubborn hearts
   to follow their own devices.

[13] "If my people would but listen to me,
   if Israel would follow my ways,
[14] how quickly would I subdue their enemies
   and turn my hand against their foes!
[15] Those who hate the LORD would cringe before him,
   and their punishment would last forever.
[16] But you would be fed with the finest of wheat;
   with honey from the rock I would satisfy you."

Open Wide

As a boy, I was always thrilled to discover a newly constructed robin's nest. It was fascinating to watch for the eggs and then to wait for those featherless little creatures with bulging eyes and gaping mouths to break out of their shells. Standing at a distance, I could see their heads bobbing unsteadily and their mouths wide open, expecting Mother Robin to give them their dinner.

As I recall those childhood scenes, I think of God's promise: "I am the LORD your God . . . Open wide your mouth, and I will fill it" (Psalm 81:10). In spite of this gracious offer to ancient Israel, the people ignored God, and He "gave them over to their stubborn hearts, to follow their own devices" (v. 12). If they had accepted God's offer, they "would be fed with the finest of wheat; with honey from the rock" (v. 16).

So too God longs to give us spiritual food. And He will satisfy our spiritual hunger as we study His Word, worship with others, listen to faithful Bible teachers, read literature with good biblical content, and daily depend on Him.

If we refuse God's provisions, we will suffer spiritual malnutrition and fail to grow. But if we open our mouth wide, we can be sure that God will fill it.

—*Richard DeHaan*

Psalm 84

¹ How lovely is your dwelling place,
    O LORD Almighty!
² My soul yearns, even faints,
    for the courts of the LORD;
 my heart and my flesh cry out
    for the living God.

³ Even the sparrow has found a home,
    and the swallow a nest for herself,
    where she may have her young—
 a place near your altar,
    O LORD Almighty, my King and my God.
⁴ Blessed are those who dwell in your house;
    they are ever praising you.   *Selah*

⁵ Blessed are those whose strength is in you,
    who have set their hearts on pilgrimage.
⁶ As they pass through the Valley of Baca,
    they make it a place of springs;
    the autumn rains also cover it with pools.
⁷ They go from strength to strength,
    till each appears before God in Zion.

⁸ Hear my prayer, O LORD God Almighty;
    listen to me, O God of Jacob.   *Selah*
⁹ Look upon our shield, O God;
    look with favor on your anointed one.

¹⁰ Better is one day in your courts
    than a thousand elsewhere;
    I would rather be a doorkeeper in the house of my God
    than dwell in the tents of the wicked.
¹¹ For the LORD God is a sun and shield;
    the LORD bestows favor and honor;
    no good thing does he withhold
    from those whose walk is blameless.

¹² O LORD Almighty,
    blessed is the man who trusts in you.

Sunshine for Your Soul

Many people feel cheerful in fair weather, but they are depressed when skies are gray. The travel industry thrives on this fact by luring millions of people to brighter climates. There's nothing wrong with enjoying the sun and its many benefits. But if we rely on good weather to maintain our good cheer, the climate of our inner world will be as changeable as the weather.

This was my condition before I became a Christian while in my teens. Each morning I would check out the weather. If it was bright, I felt happy; if it was gloomy, so was I. One night I realized I needed Jesus. Kneeling by my bed, I accepted His forgiveness for my sins and invited Him into my life. The next morning I forgot to check the weather! It simply didn't matter anymore. The "sun of righteousness" had risen in my heart (Malachi 4:2) and had replaced my fickle source of happiness with himself.

Since then, my personal world has known some dark times, but the Lord has been my constant "sun and shield" (Psalm 84:11). I still prefer sunny days, but I'm no longer a "sun-worshiper." Instead, I'm a worshiper of God's Son who shines brightly within me—whatever the weather.

—*Joanie Yoder*

Psalm 86:1–10

[1] Hear, O LORD, and answer me,
  for I am poor and needy.
[2] Guard my life, for I am devoted to you.
  You are my God; save your servant
  who trusts in you.
[3] Have mercy on me, O Lord,
  for I call to you all day long.
[4] Bring joy to your servant,
  for to you, O Lord,
  I lift up my soul.

[5] You are forgiving and good, O Lord,
  abounding in love to all who call to you.
[6] Hear my prayer, O LORD;
  listen to my cry for mercy.
[7] In the day of my trouble I will call to you,
  for you will answer me.

[8] Among the gods there is none like you, O Lord;
  no deeds can compare with yours.
[9] All the nations you have made
  will come and worship before you, O Lord;
  they will bring glory to your name.
[10] For you are great and do marvelous deeds;
  you alone are God.

Lost Prayers

The headline read: "Unanswered Prayers: Letters to God Found Dumped in Ocean."

The letters, three hundred in all and sent to a New Jersey minister, had been tossed in the ocean, most of them unopened. The minister was long dead. How the letters came to be floating in the surf off the New Jersey shore is a mystery.

The letters were addressed to the minister because he had promised to pray. Some of the letters asked for frivolous things; others were written by anguished spouses, children, or widows. They poured out their hearts to God, asking for help with relatives who were abusing drugs and alcohol or spouses who were cheating on them. One asked God for a husband and father to love her child. The reporter concluded that all were "unanswered prayers."

Not so! If those letter-writers cried out to God, He heard each one of them. Not one honest prayer is lost to His ears. "All my longings lie open before you," David wrote in the midst of a deep personal crisis, "my sighing is not hidden from you" (Psalm 38:9). David understood that we can cast all our cares on the Lord, even if no one else prays for us. He confidently concluded, "In the day of my trouble I will call to you, for you will answer me" (Psalm 86:7).

—*David Roper*

Psalm 89:5–13

⁵The heavens praise your wonders, O LORD,
   your faithfulness too, in the assembly of the holy ones.
⁶For who in the skies above can compare with the LORD?
   Who is like the LORD among the heavenly beings?
⁷In the council of the holy ones God is greatly feared;
   he is more awesome than all who surround him.
⁸O LORD God Almighty, who is like you?
   You are mighty, O LORD, and your faithfulness surrounds you.

⁹You rule over the surging sea;
   when its waves mount up, you still them.
¹⁰You crushed Rahab like one of the slain;
   with your strong arm you scattered your enemies.
¹¹The heavens are yours, and yours also the earth;
   you founded the world and all that is in it.
¹²You created the north and the south;
   Tabor and Hermon sing for joy at your name.
¹³Your arm is endued with power;
   your hand is strong, your right hand exalted.

On Loan

I am surrounded every day by things that don't belong to me, yet I call them mine. For instance, I refer to the computer I am using to write this article as "my Mac." I talk about "my office," "my desk," and "my phone." But none of this equipment belongs to me. It's mine to use, but not mine to keep. When RBC Ministries "gave" it to me, we both knew what that meant: It was on loan.

This kind of situation is not unique to employer-employee relationships. That's the way it is with all of us and all of the things we call our own. When we speak of our family, our house, or our car, we are speaking of people and things God has allowed us to enjoy while here on earth, but they really belong to Him. Notice the psalmist's praise to God, "The heavens are yours, and yours also the earth" (Psalm 89:11).

Understanding who really holds the title to all we possess should change our thinking. Just as I am aware that my employer lets me use its equipment to help me do my work more efficiently, so also should we be aware that everything we have is given to us to serve the Lord.

Our time, talents, and possessions are all on loan from God so that we can do His work effectively.

—*Dave Branon*

Psalm 90:7–17

[7] We are consumed by your anger
  and terrified by your indignation.
[8] You have set our iniquities before you,
  our secret sins in the light of your presence.
[9] All our days pass away under your wrath;
  we finish our years with a moan.
[10] The length of our days is seventy years—
  or eighty, if we have the strength;
 yet their span is but trouble and sorrow,
  for they quickly pass, and we fly away.

[11] Who knows the power of your anger?
  For your wrath is as great as the fear that is due you.
[12] Teach us to number our days aright,
  that we may gain a heart of wisdom.

[13] Relent, O LORD! How long will it be?
  Have compassion on your servants.
[14] Satisfy us in the morning with your unfailing love,
  that we may sing for joy and be glad all our days.
[15] Make us glad for as many days as you have afflicted us,
  for as many years as we have seen trouble.
[16] May your deeds be shown to your servants,
  your splendor to their children.

[17] May the favor of the Lord our God rest upon us;
  establish the work of our hands for us—
  yes, establish the work of our hands.

Eeyore Theology

How does a believer in Jesus Christ cope with life's brevity and burdens without giving in to what Michael Easley of Moody Bible Institute calls "Eeyore theology"? Eeyore, Winnie-the-Pooh's gloomy donkey friend, always walks slowly with his head down. He sees the negative side of everything. An Eeyore Christian can be heard making statements like these: "Sin is rampant everywhere—even in the church." "The world is in worse shape than ever." "God is about to judge us for our wickedness."

When Moses wrote Psalm 90, he was in a somber mood as he thought about the difference between God's eternal majesty and our human frailty. We struggle, we sorrow, we sin, we fear God, and we die (vv. 7–10). Depressing, isn't it? But Moses didn't end his psalm in that mood.

How would Moses respond to Eeyore theology? He wrote, "Satisfy us in the morning with your unfailing love, that we may sing for joy and be glad all our days!" (v. 14). When we see the value of each moment and live in the glory of our redemption and the joy of our blessings in Christ, we show our delight in God to our children and grandchildren (vv. 16–17).

Lord, keep us from being like Eeyore, and help us to leave a legacy of gladness, hope, and peace.

—Dave Egner

Psalm 91:1–12

[1] He who dwells in the shelter of the Most High
    will rest in the shadow of the Almighty.
[2] I will say of the LORD, "He is my refuge and my fortress,
    my God, in whom I trust."

[3] Surely he will save you from the fowler's snare
    and from the deadly pestilence.
[4] He will cover you with his feathers,
    and under his wings you will find refuge;
    his faithfulness will be your shield and rampart.
[5] You will not fear the terror of night,
    nor the arrow that flies by day,
[6] nor the pestilence that stalks in the darkness,
    nor the plague that destroys at midday.
[7] A thousand may fall at your side,
    ten thousand at your right hand,
    but it will not come near you.
[8] You will only observe with your eyes
    and see the punishment of the wicked.

[9] If you make the Most High your dwelling—
    even the LORD, who is my refuge—
[10] then no harm will befall you,
    no disaster will come near your tent.
[11] For he will command his angels concerning you
    to guard you in all your ways;
[12] they will lift you up in their hands,
    so that you will not strike your foot against a stone.

Frightened by a Boxer

On a bright Sunday morning one of my boys, who was just a little fellow, was walking to church with me. Soon the sights and sounds of a new day invited him to skip on ahead. Suddenly his carefree progress came to an end. A few yards away was a boxer dog looking at him. Stopping abruptly, my son turned and rushed to my side. Only when his hand was securely in mine and he knew I was right beside him was he able to walk undisturbed past the boxer.

What a picture of our pilgrimage through this world! From time to time the fierce-looking obstacles of illness, money problems, or personal conflicts appear before us, striking fear into our hearts. At first we are bewildered and life seems to be at a dead end. But then by faith we make our way to the Savior, realizing we dare not go forward without the assurance of His presence. As we completely trust in Him, He helps us face the future by walking with us each step of the way.

If anxiety and dread are lurking on the threshold of your tomorrow, remember God's wonderful promise in Isaiah 41:10, "So do not fear, for I am with you; do not be dismayed, for I am your God. I will strengthen you and help you; I will uphold you with my righteous right hand."

—*Dennis DeHaan*

Psalm 92:5–15

⁵O LORD, how great are Your works!
  Your thoughts are very deep.
⁶A senseless man does not know,
  Nor does a fool understand this.
⁷When the wicked spring up like grass,
  And when all the workers of iniquity flourish,
  It is that they may be destroyed forever.

⁸But You, LORD, are on high forevermore.
⁹For behold, Your enemies, O LORD,
  For behold, Your enemies shall perish;
  All the workers of iniquity shall be scattered.

¹⁰But my horn You have exalted like a wild ox;
  I have been anointed with fresh oil.
¹¹My eye also has seen my desire on my enemies;
  My ears hear my desire on the wicked
  Who rise up against me.

¹²The righteous shall flourish like a palm tree,
  He shall grow like a cedar in Lebanon.
¹³Those who are planted in the house of the LORD
  Shall flourish in the courts of our God.
¹⁴They shall still bear fruit in old age;
  They shall be fresh and flourishing,
¹⁵To declare that the LORD is upright;
  He is my rock, and there is no unrighteousness in Him.

(NKJV)

Growing in Old Age

We have a gnarled, ancient plum tree in our backyard that has seen better days. Its bark is dark and creased with age, its limbs are sparse and spindly, and it leans about 45 degrees to the west. Two years ago I had to cut off some branches on one side and the tree lost its symmetry.

I thought we had lost it for sure several winters ago when we had a stretch of sub-zero weather. The man who sprays our trees said he believed it was dead. Yet it came to life that spring and continues to do so every year.

Each April that old tree shrugs off the winter and puts out blossoms—fragrant pink flowers that grow profusely and beautify our yard. As I write this article, I can smell its sweetness in the air.

That plum tree endures because it has roots that tap deep into the soil. It draws its strength and nourishment from hidden subterranean sources.

And so it is with us. Our ability to endure—no, to flourish—is dependent on our being rooted in Christ. Those who read His Word, reflect on it, and pray it into their lives bring forth the fruit of the Spirit (Galatians 5:22–23), even into old age. As Psalm 92:14 says, "They shall be fresh and flourishing."

—David Roper

Psalm 93

¹The LORD reigns, he is robed in majesty;
    the LORD is robed in majesty
    and is armed with strength.
The world is firmly established;
    it cannot be moved.
²Your throne was established long ago;
    you are from all eternity.

³The seas have lifted up, O LORD,
    the seas have lifted up their voice;
    the seas have lifted up their pounding waves.
⁴Mightier than the thunder of the great waters,
    mightier than the breakers of the sea—
    the LORD on high is mighty.

⁵Your statutes stand firm;
    holiness adorns your house
    for endless days, O LORD.

Divine Mystery

At one point along the Saguenay River in southeastern Canada, the water flows through a chasm between two rugged rock formations. Their pinnacles tower over 1,600 feet into the sky. Early pioneers were so awestruck by these majestic crags that they named them Trinity and Eternity.

The two great truths expressed by these words create a sense of awe in the heart of every Christian. The Bible tells us of God's eternity—His timeless existence (Psalm 93:2) and His triune nature—the threefold expression of himself as God the Father, God the Son, and God the Holy Spirit (Matthew 28:19).

Both of these affirmations baffle our minds. If we try to comprehend either of them, the question asked by Job's friend comes to mind: "Can you fathom the mysteries of God?" (Job 11:7). The answer is obvious. When we try to behold the triune God, we feel like someone who gazes up into the midday sun to study it.

At the heart of the Christian faith is mystery, because at the heart of our faith is the eternal, triune God. We have the Father who loves us, the Savior who died for us, and the Spirit who helps us to be holy. This divine mystery gives us reason to bow down and worship our eternal God.

—*Haddon Robinson*

Psalm 94:12–23

[12] Blessed is the man you discipline, O LORD,
the man you teach from your law;
[13] you grant him relief from days of trouble,
till a pit is dug for the wicked.
[14] For the LORD will not reject his people;
he will never forsake his inheritance.
[15] Judgment will again be founded on righteousness,
and all the upright in heart will follow it.

[16] Who will rise up for me against the wicked?
Who will take a stand for me against evildoers?
[17] Unless the LORD had given me help,
I would soon have dwelt in the silence of death.
[18] When I said, "My foot is slipping,"
your love, O LORD, supported me.
[19] When anxiety was great within me,
your consolation brought joy to my soul.

[20] Can a corrupt throne be allied with you—
one that brings on misery by its decrees?
[21] They band together against the righteous
and condemn the innocent to death.
[22] But the LORD has become my fortress,
and my God the rock in whom I take refuge.
[23] He will repay them for their sins
and destroy them for their wickedness;
the LORD our God will destroy them.

Sustained in the Silence

Hudson Taylor (1832–1905) was the founder of the China Inland Mission and a great servant of God. But after the ferocious Boxer Rebellion of 1900, in which hundreds of his fellow missionaries were killed, Taylor was emotionally devastated and his health began to fail. Nearing the end of life's journey, he wrote, "I am so weak that I cannot work. I cannot read my Bible; I cannot even pray. I can only lie still in God's arms like a child and trust."

Have you been passing through a time when you are tired of body and sick of heart? Do you find it difficult to focus your mind on biblical promises? Has it become hard for you to pray? Don't write yourself off as a spiritual castaway. You are joining a host of God's people who have experienced the dark night of the soul.

When we endure such times, all we can do—indeed, all we need do—is lie still like a child in the arms of our heavenly Father. Words aren't necessary. A comforting father doesn't expect his child to make speeches. Neither does God. He knows we need His soothing care. In times of trouble, His love holds us up (Psalm 94:18). We may trust Him to carry us through that dark night of the soul and on into the dawning light.

—*Vernon Grounds*

Psalm 95

¹Come, let us sing for joy to the LORD;
    let us shout aloud to the Rock of our salvation.
²Let us come before him with thanksgiving
    and extol him with music and song.

³For the LORD is the great God,
    the great King above all gods.
⁴In his hand are the depths of the earth,
    and the mountain peaks belong to him.
⁵The sea is his, for he made it,
    and his hands formed the dry land.

⁶Come, let us bow down in worship,
    let us kneel before the LORD our Maker;
⁷for he is our God
    and we are the people of his pasture,
    the flock under his care.

  Today, if you hear his voice,
⁸do not harden your hearts as you did at Meribah,
    as you did that day at Massah in the desert,
⁹where your fathers tested and tried me,
    though they had seen what I did.
¹⁰For forty years I was angry with that generation;
    I said, "They are a people whose hearts go astray,
    and they have not known my ways."
¹¹So I declared on oath in my anger,
    "They shall never enter my rest."

We Bow Down

The ancient Greeks and Romans rejected kneeling as a part of their worship. They said that kneeling was unworthy of a free man, unsuitable for the culture of Greece, and appropriate only for barbarians. The scholars Plutarch and Theophrastus regarded kneeling as an expression of superstition. Aristotle called it a barbaric form of behavior. This belief, however, was never held by God's people.

In Psalm 95:6, the psalmist indicated that kneeling expressed a deep reverence for God. In this one verse he used three different Hebrew words to express what the attitude and position of the worshiper should be.

First, he used the word *worship*, which means to fall prostrate as a sign of honor to the Lord, with an associated meaning of allegiance to Him. The second word he used was *bow*. This means to sink down to one's knees, giving respect and worship to the Lord. The psalmist then used the word *kneel*, which means to be on one's knees giving praise to God.

According to the psalmist, kneeling in God's presence is a sign of reverence rather than a barbaric form of behavior. The important thing, however, is not just our physical position but a humble posture of the heart.

—*Marvin Williams*

Psalm 96

¹ Sing to the LORD a new song;
   sing to the LORD, all the earth.
² Sing to the LORD, praise his name;
   proclaim his salvation day after day.
³ Declare his glory among the nations,
   his marvelous deeds among all peoples.

⁴ For great is the LORD and most worthy of praise;
   he is to be feared above all gods.
⁵ For all the gods of the nations are idols,
   but the LORD made the heavens.
⁶ Splendor and majesty are before him;
   strength and glory are in his sanctuary.

⁷ Ascribe to the LORD, O families of nations,
   ascribe to the LORD glory and strength.
⁸ Ascribe to the LORD the glory due his name;
   bring an offering and come into his courts.
⁹ Worship the LORD in the splendor of his holiness;
   tremble before him, all the earth.

¹⁰ Say among the nations, "The LORD reigns."
   The world is firmly established, it cannot be moved;
   he will judge the peoples with equity.
¹¹ Let the heavens rejoice, let the earth be glad;
   let the sea resound, and all that is in it;
¹² let the fields be jubilant, and everything in them.
   Then all the trees of the forest will sing for joy;
¹³ they will sing before the LORD, for he comes,
   he comes to judge the earth.
   He will judge the world in righteousness
   and the peoples in his truth.

Daily Devotion

Tiger Woods has won many dramatic tournament victories during his professional golf career. But one of his greatest achievements went virtually unnoticed because it unfolded slowly over seven years. During that period, Tiger qualified in 142 consecutive tournaments—more than any other player in the history of U.S. professional golf. It speaks to the power of his commitment and consistency and to his conviction never to give up.

Recently I was challenged by a friend's statement of his growing desire to follow the Lord with "daily rather than dramatic devotion." Is that how it is in my life of faith in Jesus Christ? Am I consistent or erratic? Am I dependable or unreliable?

There are great spiritual events in our lives, but our daily choices to obey Christ best express our ongoing love for Him. Psalm 96, a ringing call to witness and praise, says: "Sing to the Lord, praise his name; proclaim his salvation day after day. Declare his glory among the nations, his marvelous deeds among all peoples" (vv. 2–3).

When we are consistently devoted to the Lord, we will proclaim His love and power day after day. Over time, a life of daily loyalty will become a magnificent testimony to our Savior.

—David McCasland

Psalm 97

¹ The LORD reigns, let the earth be glad;
  let the distant shores rejoice.

² Clouds and thick darkness surround him;
  righteousness and justice are the foundation of his throne.
³ Fire goes before him
  and consumes his foes on every side.
⁴ His lightning lights up the world;
  the earth sees and trembles.
⁵ The mountains melt like wax before the LORD,
  before the Lord of all the earth.
⁶ The heavens proclaim his righteousness,
  and all the peoples see his glory.

⁷ All who worship images are put to shame,
  those who boast in idols—
  worship him, all you gods!

⁸ Zion hears and rejoices
  and the villages of Judah are glad
  because of your judgments, O LORD.
⁹ For you, O LORD, are the Most High over all the earth;
  you are exalted far above all gods.

¹⁰ Let those who love the LORD hate evil,
  for he guards the lives of his faithful ones
  and delivers them from the hand of the wicked.
¹¹ Light is shed upon the righteous
  and joy on the upright in heart.
¹² Rejoice in the LORD, you who are righteous,
  and praise his holy name.

Perfect Hatred

Tell me what you hate, and I can tell you a great deal about yourself. Hatred can be the strong side of righteousness, but it needs a sign written on it with large red letters: Handle with Care.

Olive Moore, the nineteenth-century English writer, put words to this warning: "Be careful with hatred . . . Hatred is a passion requiring one hundred times the energy of love. Keep it for a cause, not an individual. Keep it for intolerance, injustice, stupidity. For hatred is the strength of the sensitive. Its power and its greatness depend on the selflessness of its use."

We tend to waste our hatred on insignificant slights and differences. Comments made by a political opponent may draw our venom. Angry letters written to the editor often raise trivia to the level of significance because of the pathology of our misdirected hatred. Churches fracture and split when hatred is directed at people and not at the forces around us that destroy life and hope.

The old Methodist circuit riders were described as men who hated nothing but sin. They took seriously the admonitions of the psalmist, "Let those who love the LORD hate evil!" (Psalm 97:10), and of the prophet Amos who urged his hearers to "hate evil, love good" (Amos 5:15).

—Haddon Robinson

Psalm 98

¹Sing to the LORD a new song,
   for he has done marvelous things;
 his right hand and his holy arm
   have worked salvation for him.
²The LORD has made his salvation known
   and revealed his righteousness to the nations.
³He has remembered his love
   and his faithfulness to the house of Israel;
   all the ends of the earth have seen
   the salvation of our God.

⁴Shout for joy to the LORD, all the earth,
   burst into jubilant song with music;
⁵make music to the LORD with the harp,
   with the harp and the sound of singing,
⁶with trumpets and the blast of the ram's horn—
   shout for joy before the LORD, the King.

⁷Let the sea resound, and everything in it,
   the world, and all who live in it.
⁸Let the rivers clap their hands,
   let the mountains sing together for joy;
⁹let them sing before the LORD,
   for he comes to judge the earth.
 He will judge the world in righteousness
   and the peoples with equity.

Music Inside

Singing comes naturally to the four von Trapp children. They are the great-grandchildren of Captain Georg von Trapp, whose romance with his second wife Maria inspired the 1965 film *The Sound of Music*.

After their grandfather Werner von Trapp had a stroke, the Montana siblings recorded their first CD in order to cheer him up. Soon the children were performing around the world. Stefan, the children's father, says, "The music is inside them."

The writer of Psalm 98 also had a song in his heart. He called on others to join him in singing "to the Lord a new song, for he has done marvelous things" (v. 1). He praised God for His salvation, His righteousness, His love, and His faithfulness (vv. 2–3). The psalmist's heart was so overflowing with praise that he called on the earth to burst into song, the rivers to clap their hands, and the mountains to be joyful (vv. 4, 8).

We have much to be thankful for as well—God's good gifts of family, friends, and His daily supply for our needs. He faithfully cares for us, His children.

We may not be able to sing well. But when we recall all that God is to us and all that He has done for us, we can't help but "burst into jubilant song" (v. 4).

—*Anne Cetas*

Psalm 99

¹The LORD reigns,
　　let the nations tremble;
　he sits enthroned between the cherubim,
　　let the earth shake.
²Great is the LORD in Zion;
　　he is exalted over all the nations.
³Let them praise your great and awesome name—
　　he is holy.

⁴The King is mighty, he loves justice—
　　you have established equity;
　in Jacob you have done
　　what is just and right.
⁵Exalt the LORD our God
　　and worship at his footstool;
　　he is holy.

⁶Moses and Aaron were among his priests,
　　Samuel was among those who called on his name;
　they called on the LORD
　　and he answered them.
⁷He spoke to them from the pillar of cloud;
　　they kept his statutes and the decrees he gave them.

⁸O LORD our God,
　　you answered them;
　you were to Israel a forgiving God,
　　though you punished their misdeeds.
⁹Exalt the LORD our God
　　and worship at his holy mountain,
　　for the LORD our God is holy.

Worthy of Worship

As Moses was tending his father-in-law's sheep in the desert, his attention was drawn to a strange sight. A bush was burning without being consumed. When Moses turned to look more closely, God said to him, "Take off your sandals, for the place where you are standing is holy ground" (Exodus 3:5).

Joshua had a similar experience when he approached the captain of the host of the Lord. As Joshua drew nearer, he was given this command: "Take off your sandals, for the place where you are standing is holy" (Joshua 5:15).

The experiences of Moses and Joshua teach us that a holy God demands our reverence and respect. True, we are encouraged to "approach the throne of grace with confidence" (Hebrews 4:16). We can enter the presence of God boldly because Jesus has opened the way for us through His death on the cross. But never are we to approach God with disrespect. Never are we to profane His name.

Our heavenly Father is not "the man upstairs." He is God, the One who is high and lifted up. And because of His majesty and holiness, we are to exalt and worship Him. As the one true God, He is worthy of our adoration. Let's give Him our highest praise.

—Richard DeHaan

Psalm 100

[1] Shout for joy to the LORD, all the earth.
[2] Worship the LORD with gladness;
    come before him with joyful songs.
[3] Know that the LORD is God.
    It is he who made us, and we are his;
    we are his people, the sheep of his pasture.

[4] Enter his gates with thanksgiving
    and his courts with praise;
    give thanks to him and praise his name.
[5] For the LORD is good and his love endures forever;
    his faithfulness continues through all generations.

God and Freedom

When members of the U.S. Second Continental Congress approved the remarkable document known as the Declaration of Independence, they plainly declared their belief in God. The drafters of this noble proclamation knew that the sweeping freedoms they were proposing could work well only in a society where the Creator is acknowledged. They affirmed that God has "endowed" all people with the right to "life, liberty, and the pursuit of happiness" because He values each of us.

Thomas Jefferson, who would become the third president of the new nation, was distressed by the sin he saw. He wrote, "I tremble for my country when I reflect that God is just." If he trembled then, he would have a violent seizure now!

The founding fathers of the United States loved the concept of individual freedom, but they did not have in mind a permissive lifestyle that allows us to do anything we please. True freedom can never be enjoyed by people who refuse to fear God.

The psalmist said, "Know that the LORD is God. It is he who made us, and we are his" (Psalm 100:3). We are responsible to God because He has created us in love.

Today, recommit yourself to living as one of God's people. That's the way to enjoy true freedom.

—*Herb VanderLugt*

Psalm 101

¹I will sing of your love and justice;
    to you, O LORD, I will sing praise.
²I will be careful to lead a blameless life—
    when will you come to me?

I will walk in my house
    with blameless heart.
³I will set before my eyes
    no vile thing.

The deeds of faithless men I hate;
    they will not cling to me.
⁴Men of perverse heart shall be far from me;
    I will have nothing to do with evil.

⁵Whoever slanders his neighbor in secret,
    him will I put to silence;
whoever has haughty eyes and a proud heart,
    him will I not endure.

⁶My eyes will be on the faithful in the land,
    that they may dwell with me;
he whose walk is blameless
    will minister to me.

⁷No one who practices deceit
    will dwell in my house;
no one who speaks falsely
    will stand in my presence.

⁸Every morning I will put to silence
    all the wicked in the land;
I will cut off every evildoer
    from the city of the LORD.

Integrity 101

Officials in Philadelphia were astonished to receive a letter and payment from a motorist who had been given a speeding ticket in 1954. John Gedge, an English tourist, had been visiting the City of Brotherly Love when he was cited for speeding. The penalty was fifteen dollars, but Gedge forgot about the ticket for almost fifty-two years until he discovered it in an old coat. "I thought, I've got to pay it," said Gedge, 84, who now lives in a nursing home in East Sussex. "Englishmen pay their debts. My conscience is clear."

This story reminded me of the psalmist David's commitment to integrity. Although he made some terrible choices in his life, Psalm 101 declares his resolve to live blamelessly. His integrity would begin in the privacy of his own house (v. 2) and extend to his choice of colleagues and friends (vv. 6–7). In sharp contrast to the corrupt lives of most kings of the ancient Near East, David's integrity led him to respect the life of his sworn enemy, King Saul (1 Samuel 24:4–6; 26:8–9).

As followers of Jesus, we are called to walk in integrity and to maintain a clear conscience. When we honor our commitments to God and to others, we will walk in fellowship with God. Our integrity will guide us (Proverbs 11:3) and help us walk securely (Proverbs 10:9).

—*Marvin Williams*

Psalm 102:1–12

¹Hear my prayer, O LORD;
    let my cry for help come to you.
²Do not hide your face from me
    when I am in distress.
Turn your ear to me;
    when I call, answer me quickly.

³For my days vanish like smoke;
    my bones burn like glowing embers.
⁴My heart is blighted and withered like grass;
    I forget to eat my food.
⁵Because of my loud groaning
    I am reduced to skin and bones.
⁶I am like a desert owl,
    like an owl among the ruins.
⁷I lie awake; I have become
    like a bird alone on a roof.
⁸All day long my enemies taunt me;
    those who rail against me use my name as a curse.
⁹For I eat ashes as my food
    and mingle my drink with tears
¹⁰because of your great wrath,
    for you have taken me up and thrown me aside.
¹¹My days are like the evening shadow;
    I wither away like grass.

¹²But you, O LORD, sit enthroned forever;
    your renown endures through all generations.

The Maker of Mountains

The Bible uses vivid imagery to express the brevity of our life on earth. Job said that his days were "swifter than a runner" and "they skim past like boats of papyrus" (Job 9:25–26).

I recall preaching at the funeral service of a young mother. From where I stood I could see the Rocky Mountains towering over the western horizon. The scene prompted me to consider how I will one day follow that friend through the valley of the shadow of death, and yet those peaks will still be thrusting themselves skyward. Eventually they will crumble into dust, but the God who made them will exist forever in undiminished glory. I also remember thinking that my deceased friend and I will, by God's grace, live with Him forever and ever.

Whenever we are troubled by the shortness of life and the impermanence of everything in this world, let's remember the Maker of the mountains. He has always been and will always be. As the psalmist said, "You, O LORD, sit enthroned forever" (Psalm 102:12).

That truth inspires us with hope. If by faith we belong to Jesus Christ the Savior, who is from everlasting to everlasting, we will one day rejoice in heaven in unending praise to Him.

—*Vernon Grounds*

Psalm 103:11–22

[11] For as high as the heavens are above the earth,
    so great is his love for those who fear him;
[12] as far as the east is from the west,
    so far has he removed our transgressions from us.
[13] As a father has compassion on his children,
    so the LORD has compassion on those who fear him;
[14] for he knows how we are formed,
    he remembers that we are dust.
[15] As for man, his days are like grass,
    he flourishes like a flower of the field;
[16] the wind blows over it and it is gone,
    and its place remembers it no more.
[17] But from everlasting to everlasting
    the LORD's love is with those who fear him,
    and his righteousness with their children's children—
[18] with those who keep his covenant
    and remember to obey his precepts.

[19] The LORD has established his throne in heaven,
    and his kingdom rules over all.

[20] Praise the LORD, you his angels,
    you mighty ones who do his bidding,
    who obey his word.
[21] Praise the LORD, all his heavenly hosts,
    you his servants who do his will.
[22] Praise the LORD, all his works
    everywhere in his dominion.

Praise the LORD, O my soul.

He Never Changes

Photographer David Crocket of Seattle's KOMO-TV knows that solid mountains can move. On May 18, 1980, he was at the foot of towering Mount St. Helens when it erupted. For ten hours he was nearly buried by the falling debris. As the atmosphere cleared, a helicopter pilot spotted him. He was dramatically rescued and flown to a hospital.

Writing about his horrendous experience, he said, "During those ten hours I saw a mountain fall apart. I saw a forest disappear . . . I saw that God is the only one who is immovable . . . I feel somehow that I'm being allowed to start over—whatever is in His master plan for me."

Nothing in our world, not even a mountain, is absolutely indestructible. God alone is absolutely unchangeable—He endures "forever" (Psalm 102:12). He "has established his throne in heaven, and his kingdom rules over all" (Psalm 103:19).

When we trust ourselves to God's keeping, we are forever secure. He removes our sins from us "as far as the east is from the west" (Psalm 103:12). And His love toward us is "from everlasting to everlasting" (v. 17). He holds us in His almighty hands, and nothing can pry us loose from that omnipotent grip (John 10:28–29).

—Vernon Grounds

Psalm 104:31–35

[31] May the glory of the LORD endure forever;
    may the LORD rejoice in his works—
[32] he who looks at the earth, and it trembles,
    who touches the mountains, and they smoke.
[33] I will sing to the LORD all my life;
    I will sing praise to my God as long as I live.
[34] May my meditation be pleasing to him,
    as I rejoice in the LORD.
[35] But may sinners vanish from the earth
    and the wicked be no more.

Praise the LORD, O my soul.

Praise the LORD.

The Universe Is God's

Rising 6.3 miles from its base on the ocean floor and stretching 75 miles across, Hawaii's Mauna Loa is the largest volcano on Earth. But on the surface of the planet Mars stands Olympus Mons, the largest volcano yet discovered in our solar system. The altitude of Olympus Mons is three times higher than Mt. Everest and 100 times more massive than Mauna Loa. It's large enough to contain the entire chain of the Hawaiian Islands!

Long ago, David looked up at the night skies and stood in awe at the wonder of his Creator's universe. He wrote, "The heavens declare the glory of God; the skies proclaim the work of his hands" (Psalm 19:1).

But the stars and the sky were not all that stirred the wonder of ancient writers. Earthquakes and volcanoes also inspired awe for the Creator. Psalm 104 says, "[God] looks at the earth, and it trembles, [He] touches the mountains, and they smoke" (v. 32).

As space probes explore more of our solar system, they will continue to discover unknown wonders. But whatever they find is the work of the same Creator (Genesis 1:1).

The wonders of the universe should move us to praise God, just as they moved a shepherd boy long ago as he gazed up at the heavens (Psalm 8:3–5).

—*Dennis Fisher*

Psalm 106:1–15

[1] Praise the LORD.

Give thanks to the LORD, for he is good;
    his love endures forever.
[2] Who can proclaim the mighty acts of the LORD
    or fully declare his praise?
[3] Blessed are they who maintain justice,
    who constantly do what is right.
[4] Remember me, O LORD, when you show favor to your people,
    come to my aid when you save them,
[5] that I may enjoy the prosperity of your chosen ones,
    that I may share in the joy of your nation
    and join your inheritance in giving praise.

[6] We have sinned, even as our fathers did;
    we have done wrong and acted wickedly.
[7] When our fathers were in Egypt,
    they gave no thought to your miracles;
    they did not remember your many kindnesses,
    and they rebelled by the sea, the Red Sea.
[8] Yet he saved them for his name's sake,
    to make his mighty power known.
[9] He rebuked the Red Sea, and it dried up;
    he led them through the depths as through a desert.
[10] He saved them from the hand of the foe;
    from the hand of the enemy he redeemed them.
[11] The waters covered their adversaries;
    not one of them survived.
[12] Then they believed his promises
    and sang his praise.

[13] But they soon forgot what he had done
    and did not wait for his counsel.
[14] In the desert they gave in to their craving;
    in the wasteland they put God to the test.
[15] So he gave them what they asked for,
    but sent a wasting disease upon them.

Beware of Quick Fixes

Some people pray only in a crisis. They have a "quick fix" mentality that sees God mainly as a problem solver. When merciful solutions come, He is courteously thanked, then more or less forgotten until the next crisis.

The story is told of a young rich girl, accustomed to servants, who was afraid to climb a dark stairway alone. Her mother suggested that she overcome her fear by asking Jesus to go with her up the stairs. When the child reached the top, she was overheard saying, "Thank you, Jesus. You may go now."

We may smile at that story, but Psalm 106 contains a serious warning against dismissing God from our lives—as if that were possible. Israel took the Lord's mercies for granted, and God called that rebellion (v. 7). They developed malnourished souls because they chose to ignore Him (vv. 13–15). What a lesson for us!

Anticipate great things from God, but don't expect Him to come at your beck and call. Instead, be at His beck and call, eager to fulfill His will.

Like the little rich girl, ask God to accompany you through life's dark passageways. But instead of dismissing Him when your special needs are met, cling to Him as if your life depended on it. It does!

—*Joanie Yoder*

Psalm 107:1–9

[1] Give thanks to the LORD, for he is good;
  his love endures forever.
[2] Let the redeemed of the LORD say this—
  those he redeemed from the hand of the foe,
[3] those he gathered from the lands,
  from east and west, from north and south.
[4] Some wandered in desert wastelands,
  finding no way to a city where they could settle.
[5] They were hungry and thirsty,
  and their lives ebbed away.
[6] Then they cried out to the LORD in their trouble,
  and he delivered them from their distress.
[7] He led them by a straight way
  to a city where they could settle.
[8] Let them give thanks to the LORD for his unfailing love
  and his wonderful deeds for men,
[9] for he satisfies the thirsty
  and fills the hungry with good things.

Rescue and Response

The sign outside Dave James's shop in Seattle, Washington, says more about getting your life repaired than it does about fixing your vacuum cleaner, but Dave is in business to do both. The top line of the sign is always the same: Free Bibles Inside. The second line changes and features thoughts such as: Surrender Your Heart for a Brand-New Start.

Over the past decade, Mr. James has repaired thousands of vacuum cleaners and given away thousands of Bibles to his customers. It's his way of saying thanks to the Lord for saving him from destruction.

As a successful businessman, Dave James had slipped into a life of drug addiction. "If God hadn't taken cocaine away from me," he says, "I'd be dead." The Lord helped him get clean and find a new beginning.

Every testimony for Christ begins with a rescue followed by a thankful response: "Give thanks to the LORD, for he is good; his love endures forever" (Psalm 107:1).

Whether our experience of salvation sounds dramatic or not, the reality remains: "He has rescued us from the dominion of darkness and brought us into the kingdom of the Son he loves" (Colossians 1:13). Because we have been redeemed, we should want to tell others.

—David McCasland

Psalm 108

[1] My heart is steadfast, O God;
   I will sing and make music with all my soul.
[2] Awake, harp and lyre!
   I will awaken the dawn.
[3] I will praise you, O LORD, among the nations;
   I will sing of you among the peoples.
[4] For great is your love, higher than the heavens;
   your faithfulness reaches to the skies.
[5] Be exalted, O God, above the heavens,
   and let your glory be over all the earth.

[6] Save us and help us with your right hand,
   that those you love may be delivered.
[7] God has spoken from his sanctuary:
   "In triumph I will parcel out Shechem
   and measure off the Valley of Succoth.
[8] Gilead is mine, Manasseh is mine;
   Ephraim is my helmet,
   Judah my scepter.
[9] Moab is my washbasin,
   upon Edom I toss my sandal;
   over Philistia I shout in triumph."

[10] Who will bring me to the fortified city?
   Who will lead me to Edom?
[11] Is it not you, O God, you who have rejected us
   and no longer go out with our armies?
[12] Give us aid against the enemy,
   for the help of man is worthless.
[13] With God we will gain the victory,
   and he will trample down our enemies.

Now's Your Chance, Lord!

John and Betty Stam, the famous missionaries to China who were martyred for the cause of Christ, had led a young girl to the Lord and later hired her to do their housework. Although converted, she had some serious problems for which there seemed to be no solution.

One day, in deep distress, she went to her bedroom and cried out to the Savior for help. John and Betty overheard her and were deeply moved. They were especially touched when she said with the utmost reverence and faith, "Now's your chance, Lord! Now's your chance!" Her earnest prayers were rewarded, for God soon helped her solve her problems.

Someone has said, "There are two ways of getting help in time of need. One is to go around to all your friends and be disappointed, and then as a last resort turn to the Lord. The other is to take a shortcut and go to Him first. Don't make a move until you have first expressed your need to Him!"

Are you standing at "wits'-end corner," without any solution to your problems in sight? Pour out your heart to the Lord. Tell Him you are unable to cope with your desperate situation. Then wait patiently for His help. He will provide the answer at just the right moment.

—*Henry Bosch*

Psalm 111

¹Praise the LORD.

I will extol the LORD with all my heart
   in the council of the upright and in the assembly.

²Great are the works of the LORD;
   they are pondered by all who delight in them.
³Glorious and majestic are his deeds,
   and his righteousness endures forever.
⁴He has caused his wonders to be remembered;
   the LORD is gracious and compassionate.
⁵He provides food for those who fear him;
   he remembers his covenant forever.
⁶He has shown his people the power of his works,
   giving them the lands of other nations.
⁷The works of his hands are faithful and just;
   all his precepts are trustworthy.
⁸They are steadfast for ever and ever,
   done in faithfulness and uprightness.
⁹He provided redemption for his people;
   he ordained his covenant forever—
   holy and awesome is his name.

¹⁰The fear of the LORD is the beginning of wisdom;
   all who follow his precepts have good understanding.
   To him belongs eternal praise.

Out of Proportion

I'll never forget the time I had my picture taken with Shaquille O'Neal, one of the giants of professional basketball. I never thought of myself as short until I stood next to his 7'1" frame. With my head tucked under his arm, I suddenly realized that I wasn't as tall as I thought I was, at least not when standing next to the Shaq!

The psalmist wrote, "The fear of the LORD is the beginning of wisdom" (Psalm 111:10). Fearing God requires that we get things in the proper proportion, like the fact that He is so much greater in every way than we are. "Great are the works of the LORD" (v. 2). They are the outworking of His love, strength, wisdom, foresight, will, and faithfulness. Fearing God means coming to grips with this truth.

But it's easy to miss the point when we don't stay close to God. The closer we get to Him, the more we realize how much we are lacking and how desperately we need His far greater wisdom to direct our lives. Left to our little selves, we get everything out of sync. If we're honest, we have to admit that our limited perspective is often wrong and sometimes can be destructive.

Wise people realize how little they know and how much they need the great wisdom of God.

—*Joe Stowell*

Psalm 112

¹ Praise the LORD.

Blessed is the man who fears the LORD,
who finds great delight in his commands.

² His children will be mighty in the land;
the generation of the upright will be blessed.
³ Wealth and riches are in his house,
and his righteousness endures forever.
⁴ Even in darkness light dawns for the upright,
for the gracious and compassionate and righteous man.
⁵ Good will come to him who is generous and lends freely,
who conducts his affairs with justice.
⁶ Surely he will never be shaken;
a righteous man will be remembered forever.
⁷ He will have no fear of bad news;
his heart is steadfast, trusting in the LORD.
⁸ His heart is secure, he will have no fear;
in the end he will look in triumph on his foes.
⁹ He has scattered abroad his gifts to the poor,
his righteousness endures forever;
his horn will be lifted high in honor.

¹⁰ The wicked man will see and be vexed,
he will gnash his teeth and waste away;
the longings of the wicked will come to nothing.

Bad News?

Several years ago, before cell phones became common, a seminar leader asked the audience, "If someone came into this meeting, called your name, and said, 'You have a phone call,' would you assume that it was good news or bad news?" Most of us admitted we would think it was bad news, but we weren't sure why.

It points out a common burden many people carry—the fear of bad news. It may be a natural concern for the safety of those we love, but it can become an irrational dread of tragedy.

When we are most afraid, we most need confidence in God. Psalm 112 speaks of a person who fears the Lord, delights in His commandments, and is gracious to others (vv. 1, 4–5). But perhaps most striking is: "He will have no fear of bad news; his heart is steadfast, trusting in the LORD" (v. 7).

A hymn by Frances Havergal reminds us that a trusting heart is the answer for a worried mind: "Stayed upon Jehovah, hearts are fully blest; finding, as He promised, perfect peace and rest."

The Bible doesn't promise that we will never receive bad news. But it does assure us that we don't have to live each day in gnawing fear of what might happen. "His heart is secure; he will have no fear" (v. 8).

—David McCasland

Psalm 116:8–19

[8] For you, O LORD, have delivered my soul from death,
    my eyes from tears,
    my feet from stumbling,
[9] that I may walk before the LORD
    in the land of the living.
[10] I believed; therefore I said,
    "I am greatly afflicted."
[11] And in my dismay I said,
    "All men are liars."

[12] How can I repay the LORD
    for all his goodness to me?
[13] I will lift up the cup of salvation
    and call on the name of the LORD.
[14] I will fulfill my vows to the LORD
    in the presence of all his people.

[15] Precious in the sight of the LORD
    is the death of his saints.
[16] O LORD, truly I am your servant;
    I am your servant, the son of your maidservant;
    you have freed me from my chains.

[17] I will sacrifice a thank offering to you
    and call on the name of the LORD.
[18] I will fulfill my vows to the LORD
    in the presence of all his people,
[19] in the courts of the house of the LORD—
    in your midst, O Jerusalem.

Praise the LORD.

God Weeps with Us

What is the meaning of Psalm 116:15, "Precious in the sight of the LORD is the death of his saints"? God certainly doesn't value or find enjoyment in the death of His children! If He did, why would the psalmist praise God for delivering him from death? And why did Jesus groan and weep as He saw the grief at Lazarus' tomb? (John 11:33–35). I agree with scholars who render Psalm 116:15, "*Costly* in the sight of the Lord is the death of His saints."

In this world, unless you are a celebrity, your passing will soon be forgotten by all but a small circle of relatives and friends. But Jesus showed us that God shares the sorrow and pain of the bereaved and that the death of the humblest believer causes His heart great pain.

This thought came to me recently at the funeral of my brother Tunis. His family and his pastor extolled his compassion, kindness, and generosity. Afterward, people who knew him as a businessman spoke well of him. Though his name was just one of many in the newspaper obituaries, his death was a matter of great loss to us who knew and loved him. And it is comforting to know that God did not take his passing without feeling our pain. In fact, I believe He wept with us.

—Herb VanderLugt

Psalm 118:1–7; 22–29

[1] Give thanks to the LORD, for he is good;
　　his love endures forever.

[2] Let Israel say:
　　"His love endures forever."
[3] Let the house of Aaron say:
　　"His love endures forever."
[4] Let those who fear the LORD say:
　　"His love endures forever."

[5] In my anguish I cried to the LORD,
　　and he answered by setting me free.
[6] The LORD is with me; I will not be afraid.
　　What can man do to me?
[7] The LORD is with me; he is my helper.
　　I will look in triumph on my enemies.

[22] The stone the builders rejected
　　has become the capstone;
[23] the LORD has done this,
　　and it is marvelous in our eyes.
[24] This is the day the LORD has made;
　　let us rejoice and be glad in it.

[25] O LORD, save us;
　　O LORD, grant us success.
[26] Blessed is he who comes in the name of the LORD.
　　From the house of the LORD we bless you.
[27] The LORD is God,
　　and he has made his light shine upon us.
　With boughs in hand, join in the festal procession
　　up to the horns of the altar.

[28] You are my God, and I will give you thanks;
　　you are my God, and I will exalt you.

[29] Give thanks to the LORD, for he is good;
　　his love endures forever.

Have a Great Day!

I was in a convenience store one day, standing in line behind a man paying for his groceries. When he was finished, the clerk sent him off with a cheery "Have a great day!"

To the clerk's surprise (and mine) the man exploded in anger. "This is one of the worst days of my life," he shouted. "How can I have a great day?" And with that he stormed out of the store.

I understand the man's frustration; I too have "bad" days over which I have no control. *How can I have a great day,* I ask myself, *when it's beyond my control?* Then I remember these words: "This is the day the LORD has made" (Psalm 118:24).

The Lord has made every day, and my Father will show himself strong on my behalf today. He has control over everything in it—even the hard things that will come my way. All events have been screened through His wisdom and love, and they are opportunities for me to grow in faith. "His love endures forever" (v. 1). "The Lord is with me; I will not be afraid" (v. 6).

Now, when people give me the parting admonition to have a great day, I reply, "That's beyond my control, but I can be grateful for whatever comes my way and rejoice—for this is the day the Lord has made."

—*David Roper*

Psalm 119:9–16

⁹ How can a young man keep his way pure?
   By living according to your word.
¹⁰ I seek you with all my heart;
   do not let me stray from your commands.
¹¹ I have hidden your word in my heart
   that I might not sin against you.
¹² Praise be to you, O LORD;
   teach me your decrees.
¹³ With my lips I recount
   all the laws that come from your mouth.
¹⁴ I rejoice in following your statutes
   as one rejoices in great riches.
¹⁵ I meditate on your precepts
   and consider your ways.
¹⁶ I delight in your decrees;
   I will not neglect your word.

Something for the Soul

Filled to the brim with inspiring anecdotes and stories, the books in the *Chicken Soup for the Soul* series quickly became bestsellers. It's no wonder. A title that includes "chicken soup" brings back memories of childhood, stuffed-up noses, and scratchy throats—a time when only a warm blanket and Mom's steaming chicken and rice soup will bring about relief.

Scientific evidence now indicates that Mom was pretty smart. Chicken soup is beneficial for fighting colds. It's also one of the foods that people describe as "comfort food."

When it's not my body but my heart that is aching, I long for the comfort of God's Word: soothing words like "Cast all your anxiety on him because he cares for you" (1 Peter 5:7); assuring words that nothing can "separate us from the love of God that is in Christ Jesus our Lord" (Romans 8:39).

The Bible—the world's all-time bestseller—is filled with promises, reminders, challenges, and knowledge of God. When you're feeling discouraged, try ladling up a big serving of God's Word. Having a Bible within reach (or better yet, Scripture hidden in your heart) infinitely trumps a bowl of Mom's chicken soup. It will warm your heart and begin your healing.

—*Cindy Hess Kasper*

Psalm 121

¹I lift up my eyes to the hills—
    where does my help come from?
²My help comes from the LORD,
    the Maker of heaven and earth.

³He will not let your foot slip—
    he who watches over you will not slumber;
⁴indeed, he who watches over Israel
    will neither slumber nor sleep.

⁵The LORD watches over you—
    the LORD is your shade at your right hand;
⁶the sun will not harm you by day,
    nor the moon by night.

⁷The LORD will keep you from all harm—
    he will watch over your life;
⁸the LORD will watch over your coming and going
    both now and forevermore.

Always Awake

A mother and her four-year-old daughter were preparing for bed. The child was afraid of the dark. When the lights were turned off, the girl noticed the moon shining through the window. "Mommy," she asked, "is that God's light up there?"

"Yes, it is," came the reply.

Soon another question: "Will He put it out and go to sleep too?"

"Oh no, He never goes to sleep."

After a few silent moments, the little girl said, "As long as God is awake, I'm not scared." Realizing that the Lord would be watching over her, the reassured child soon fell into a peaceful sleep.

As Christians, we may confidently commit both the night and the day to our ever-faithful God. He is fully aware of our fears in the dark as well as our frustrations in the light. We can be assured of His constant care. His loving eye and protecting hand are always upon us.

Perhaps you face lonely hours because of illness or the loss of a loved one. The shadows of the night make the anxiety of your situation seem greater than ever. Doubts arise and fears flood your soul, robbing you of your needed rest.

Trust the heavenly Father, and with the psalmist you will be able to say, "I will lie down and sleep in peace, for you alone, O LORD, make me dwell in safety" (Psalm 4:8).

Remember, God is always awake.

—Paul Van Gorder

Psalm 122

[1] I rejoiced with those who said to me,
  "Let us go to the house of the LORD."
[2] Our feet are standing
  in your gates, O Jerusalem.

[3] Jerusalem is built like a city
  that is closely compacted together.
[4] That is where the tribes go up,
  the tribes of the LORD,
  to praise the name of the LORD
  according to the statute given to Israel.
[5] There the thrones for judgment stand,
  the thrones of the house of David.

[6] Pray for the peace of Jerusalem:
  "May those who love you be secure.
[7] May there be peace within your walls
  and security within your citadels."
[8] For the sake of my brothers and friends,
  I will say, "Peace be within you."
[9] For the sake of the house of the LORD our God,
  I will seek your prosperity.

Mrs. Craig's Problem

Church attendance is a privilege. We recognize that some people cannot attend because of physical problems or other legitimate reasons. But those who can be in church should be. The singing, prayers, fellowship, and teaching of God's Word are just what we need for the week ahead.

The *Nashville Banner* reported that 81-year-old Ella Craig had perfect attendance in Sunday school for twenty years. That's 1,040 Sundays! The article then raised these questions:

1. Doesn't Mrs. Craig ever have company on Sunday to keep her away from church?
2. Doesn't she ever have headaches, colds, nervous spells, or tired feelings?
3. Doesn't she ever take a weekend trip?
4. Doesn't she ever sleep late on Sunday morning?
5. Doesn't it ever rain or snow on Sunday morning?
6. Doesn't she ever get her feelings hurt by someone in the church?

The article concluded by asking, "What's the matter with Mrs. Craig?" The answer? Nothing at all. But if we are not in church on Sunday when we can be, there is something wrong with us! We need to take a lesson from Mrs. Craig.

—*Richard DeHaan*

Psalm 126

¹When the LORD brought back the captives to Zion,
we were like men who dreamed.
²Our mouths were filled with laughter,
our tongues with songs of joy.
Then it was said among the nations,
"The LORD has done great things for them."
³The LORD has done great things for us,
and we are filled with joy.

⁴Restore our fortunes, O LORD,
like streams in the Negev.
⁵Those who sow in tears
will reap with songs of joy.
⁶He who goes out weeping,
carrying seed to sow,
will return with songs of joy,
carrying sheaves with him.

What's in Your Mouth?

Communications experts tell us that the average person speaks enough to fill twenty single-spaced, typewritten pages every day. This means our mouths crank out enough words to fill two books of three hundred pages each month, twenty-four books each year, and twelve hundred books in fifty years of speaking. Thanks to phones, voicemail, and face-to-face conversations, words comprise a large part of our lives. So the kinds of words we use are important.

The psalmist's mouth was filled with praise when he wrote Psalm 126. The Lord had done great things for him and his people. Even the nations around them noticed. Remembering God's blessings, he said, "Our mouths were filled with laughter, our tongues with songs of joy" (v. 2).

What words would you have used in verse 3 had you been writing this psalm? So often our attitude seems to be: "The Lord has done great things for me, and I—

. . . can't recall any of them right now."

. . . am wondering what He'll do for me next."

. . . need much more."

Or can you finish it by saying, "and I am praising and thanking Him for His goodness"? As you recall God's blessings today, express your words of praise to Him.

—*Anne Cetas*

Psalm 127

[1] Unless the LORD builds the house,
    its builders labor in vain.
    Unless the LORD watches over the city,
    the watchmen stand guard in vain.
[2] In vain you rise early
    and stay up late,
    toiling for food to eat—
    for he grants sleep to those he loves.

[3] Sons are a heritage from the LORD,
    children a reward from him.
[4] Like arrows in the hands of a warrior
    are sons born in one's youth.
[5] Blessed is the man
    whose quiver is full of them.
 They will not be put to shame
    when they contend with their enemies in the gate.

Fine Crystal

I have a friend—call her Mary—who tells me that her fondest memory is of the morning she broke her mother's "priceless" crystal.

Mary's mother was having a party. She had taken her fine crystal from the cupboard and carefully washed it and placed it on the table. The crystal represented the only valuable material possession her mother owned, and it was used only on special occasions.

In her rush to get things ready for her guests, Mary's mother said to her young daughter, "Would you please find some place that's not underfoot?" So Mary crawled underneath the table. Unfortunately, she kicked the leg of the table and the crystal crashed to the floor.

"Crystal exploded like shrapnel," she recalls. She had destroyed the most elegant thing her mother possessed. "I'm so sorry," the little girl sobbed.

Her mother gathered her in her arms and whispered, "Don't cry, honey. You are far more valuable to me than mere crystal."

Children are indeed our most valuable possession, more precious than anything we could ever buy or earn. They are "a heritage from the LORD" and "a reward" (Psalm 127:3).

Do your children know how precious they are to you? Why not tell them today.

—David Roper

Psalm 130

¹Out of the depths I cry to you, O LORD;
²   O Lord, hear my voice.
Let your ears be attentive
    to my cry for mercy.

³If you, O LORD, kept a record of sins,
    O Lord, who could stand?
⁴But with you there is forgiveness;
    therefore you are feared.

⁵I wait for the LORD, my soul waits,
    and in his word I put my hope.
⁶My soul waits for the Lord
    more than watchmen wait for the morning,
    more than watchmen wait for the morning.

⁷O Israel, put your hope in the LORD,
    for with the LORD is unfailing love
    and with him is full redemption.
⁸He himself will redeem Israel
    from all their sins.

Forgiven

God is highly dangerous. We are sinful and He is holy. Sin can no more exist in the presence of God than darkness can exist in the presence of light. To stand before Him in self-righteousness would be to invite our destruction. The psalmist wrote, "If you, O LORD, kept a record of sins, O LORD, who could stand?" (Psalm 130:3).

In a cemetery not far from New York City is a headstone engraved with a single word: *Forgiven*. The message is simple and unembellished. There is no date of birth, no date of death, no epitaph. There is only a name and the solitary word *forgiven*. But that is the greatest word that could ever be applied to any man or woman or that could be written on any gravestone.

The songwriter said, "But with you there is forgiveness; therefore you are feared" (v. 4). That refrain echoes in both the Old and New Testaments. God is honored and worshiped because He alone can clear our record.

If God could not forgive us, we could only flee from Him in terror. Yet the God whose holiness threatens us is the God who through Christ redeems us. This dangerous God offers forgiveness for all our sins. We only need to ask Him.

Are you forgiven?

—Haddon Robinson

Psalm 138

[1] I will praise you, O LORD, with all my heart;
    before the "gods" I will sing your praise.
[2] I will bow down toward your holy temple
    and will praise your name
    for your love and your faithfulness,
 for you have exalted above all things
    your name and your word.
[3] When I called, you answered me;
    you made me bold and stouthearted.

[4] May all the kings of the earth praise you, O LORD,
    when they hear the words of your mouth.
[5] May they sing of the ways of the LORD,
    for the glory of the LORD is great.

[6] Though the LORD is on high, he looks upon the lowly,
    but the proud he knows from afar.
[7] Though I walk in the midst of trouble,
    you preserve my life;
you stretch out your hand against the anger of my foes,
    with your right hand you save me.
[8] The LORD will fulfill his purpose for me;
    your love, O LORD, endures forever—
    do not abandon the works of your hands.

Facing My Fears

After Bill and I married, I became overly dependent on him rather than depending on God for my security and strength. Feeling very inadequate and fearful, secretly I worried, "What if one day I don't have Bill any more?"

When our missionary work took Bill from home for weeks at a time, I began to depend on myself instead of Bill. Feeling even more inadequate, I reduced the risks of life whenever possible and lived within a cocoon of anxiety, even being afraid to go out in public.

Finally, at rock bottom, I followed David's example in Psalm 138:3. He said, "When I called, you answered me; you made me bold and stouthearted." I too cried out and God answered me. His answer gave me the understanding and strength to crack open the cocoon of fear and begin spreading my wings in dependence on God. Slowly but surely He made me a bold servant at Bill's side.

Years later, when Bill died, I recognized how compassionately God had dealt with my earlier fear: "What if one day I don't have Bill any more?" Instead of removing my fear, God gave me the strength and ability to face it. And He will enable you as you depend on Him.

—*Joanie Yoder*

Psalm 139:1–12

¹O LORD, you have searched me
and you know me.
²You know when I sit and when I rise;
you perceive my thoughts from afar.
³You discern my going out and my lying down;
you are familiar with all my ways.
⁴Before a word is on my tongue
you know it completely, O LORD.

⁵You hem me in—behind and before;
you have laid your hand upon me.
⁶Such knowledge is too wonderful for me,
too lofty for me to attain.

⁷Where can I go from your Spirit?
Where can I flee from your presence?
⁸If I go up to the heavens, you are there;
if I make my bed in the depths, you are there.
⁹If I rise on the wings of the dawn,
if I settle on the far side of the sea,
¹⁰even there your hand will guide me,
your right hand will hold me fast.

¹¹If I say, "Surely the darkness will hide me
and the light become night around me,"
¹²even the darkness will not be dark to you;
the night will shine like the day,
for darkness is as light to you.

He Is There

Tanya's fiancé David was lying in the intensive care unit after a delicate procedure to repair a brain aneurysm. David's eyes focused on Tanya, who had hardly left his side in several days. In wonder, he said, "Every time I look up, you're here. I love that. Every time I think of you, I open my eyes and you are there."

That young man's appreciation for the woman he loves reminds me of the way we should feel about God's presence in our lives.

He is always there. The Lord's presence gives us comfort and security. He has promised that He will never leave us or forsake us (Hebrews 13:5). Who knows us more completely? Who loves us more fully? Who cares for us so well?

In Psalm 139, we read what King David thought of God's precious presence. He wrote, "O Lord, you have searched me and you know me. You know when I sit and when I rise; . . . you are familiar with all my ways . . . If I go up to the heavens, you are there" (vv. 1– 3, 8).

No matter what happens to us, we have this assurance: "God is our refuge and strength, an ever-present help in trouble" (Psalm 46:1). Open your eyes and your heart. He is there.

—*Cindy Hess Kasper*

Psalm 141

[1] O LORD, I call to you; come quickly to me.
    Hear my voice when I call to you.
[2] May my prayer be set before you like incense;
    may the lifting up of my hands be like the evening sacrifice.

[3] Set a guard over my mouth, O LORD;
    keep watch over the door of my lips.
[4] Let not my heart be drawn to what is evil,
    to take part in wicked deeds
 with men who are evildoers;
    let me not eat of their delicacies.

[5] Let a righteous man strike me—it is a kindness;
    let him rebuke me—it is oil on my head.
    My head will not refuse it.

 Yet my prayer is ever against the deeds of evildoers;
[6]   their rulers will be thrown down from the cliffs,
    and the wicked will learn that my words were well spoken.
[7] They will say, "As one plows and breaks up the earth,
    so our bones have been scattered at the mouth of the grave."
[8] But my eyes are fixed on you, O Sovereign LORD;
    in you I take refuge—do not give me over to death.
[9] Keep me from the snares they have laid for me,
    from the traps set by evildoers.
[10] Let the wicked fall into their own nets,
    while I pass by in safety.

Cracked Lenses

I started wearing glasses when I was ten years old. They are still a necessity because my fifty-something eyes are losing their battle against time. When I was younger, I thought glasses were a nuisance—especially when playing sports. Once, the lenses of my glasses got cracked while I was playing softball. It took several weeks to get them replaced. In the meantime, I saw everything in a skewed and distorted way.

In life, pain often functions like cracked lenses. It creates within us a conflict between what we experience and what we believe. Pain can give us a badly distorted perspective on life—and on God. In those times, we need our God to provide us with new lenses to help us see clearly again. That clarity of sight usually begins when we turn our eyes upon the Lord. The psalmist encouraged us to do this: "My eyes are fixed on you, O Sovereign LORD; in you I take refuge" (Psalm 141:8). Seeing God clearly can help us see life's experiences more clearly.

As we turn our eyes to the Lord in times of pain and struggle, we will experience His comfort and hope in our daily lives. He will help us to see everything clearly again.

—*Bill Crowder*

Psalm 142

¹I cry aloud to the LORD;
    I lift up my voice to the LORD for mercy.
²I pour out my complaint before him;
    before him I tell my trouble.

³When my spirit grows faint within me,
    it is you who know my way.
In the path where I walk
    men have hidden a snare for me.
⁴Look to my right and see;
    no one is concerned for me.
I have no refuge;
    no one cares for my life.

⁵I cry to you, O LORD;
    I say, "You are my refuge,
    my portion in the land of the living."
⁶Listen to my cry,
    for I am in desperate need;
rescue me from those who pursue me,
    for they are too strong for me.
⁷Set me free from my prison,
    that I may praise your name.

Then the righteous will gather about me
    because of your goodness to me.

Dave Man

David was stuck in a cave, as the note at the beginning of this particular psalm tells us. Some Bible commentators think this was when he was running from King Saul, who wanted to kill him (1 Samuel 22:1). Trouble and trouble-makers hounded him. Hemmed in by his circumstances and smothered by danger, he turned to God for help.

> David was frightened, so he poured out his complaint to God (v. 2).
> He felt alone and uncared for, so he cried out to God (vv. 1, 4–5).
> His situation was desperate, so he pleaded for rescue (v. 6).
> David was trapped, so he begged for freedom (v. 7).

What cave surrounds you today? A cave of despair brought on by grief or illness? A cave of difficulties caused by your own poor decisions? Are you stuck in a cave of questions or doubts that rob you of joy and confidence?

Here's what David did when he was trapped in his cave: He asked God for mercy, he sought refuge in Him, and he promised to use his eventual freedom as a way to praise God. In the end, he looked forward to the comfort of fellow believers.

Complaint followed by faith. Desperation followed by praise. Loneliness followed by fellowship. We can learn a lot from a cave man.

—*Dave Branon*

Psalm 143:4–12

4 So my spirit grows faint within me;
    my heart within me is dismayed.

5 I remember the days of long ago;
    I meditate on all your works
    and consider what your hands have done.
6 I spread out my hands to you;
    my soul thirsts for you like a parched land.   *Selah*

7 Answer me quickly, O LORD;
    my spirit fails.
 Do not hide your face from me
    or I will be like those who go down to the pit.
8 Let the morning bring me word of your unfailing love,
    for I have put my trust in you.
 Show me the way I should go,
    for to you I lift up my soul.
9 Rescue me from my enemies, O LORD,
    for I hide myself in you.
10 Teach me to do your will,
    for you are my God;
 may your good Spirit
    lead me on level ground.

11 For your name's sake, O LORD, preserve my life;
    in your righteousness, bring me out of trouble.
12 In your unfailing love, silence my enemies;
    destroy all my foes,
    for I am your servant.

Thoughtful Praises

Most of us long to praise God more joyfully than we do. One common hindrance is that no matter how hard we try, we often don't feel like praising Him.

Bible teacher Selwyn Hughes says that God has placed within us three main functions: the will, the feelings, and the thoughts. Our will, he says, has little or no power over our feelings. You can't say, "I am going to feel different" and then accomplish it by sheer willpower. What the feelings do respond to are the thoughts. Quoting another source, Hughes says: "Our feelings follow our thoughts like baby ducks follow their mother." So how can we make our thoughts the leader of our feelings?

David showed us the way in Psalm 143. Feeling overwhelmed and distressed (v. 4), he took time to think about the Lord (v. 5). He remembered God's lovingkindness, trustworthiness, and guidance (v. 8); His protection and goodness (vv. 9–10); His righteousness and unfailing love (vv. 11–12). Once David got going, his feelings began to follow his thoughts.

Name your own blessings daily; contemplate them thoroughly; speak about them to God and to others. Gradually your concern about feelings will diminish and you'll be praising God with joy.

—*Joanie Yoder*

Psalm 144:9–15

⁹ I will sing a new song to you, O God;
   on the ten-stringed lyre I will make music to you,
¹⁰ to the One who gives victory to kings,
   who delivers his servant David from the deadly sword.

¹¹ Deliver me and rescue me
   from the hands of foreigners
whose mouths are full of lies,
   whose right hands are deceitful.

¹² Then our sons in their youth
   will be like well-nurtured plants,
and our daughters will be like pillars
   carved to adorn a palace.
¹³ Our barns will be filled
   with every kind of provision.
Our sheep will increase by thousands,
   by tens of thousands in our fields;
¹⁴   our oxen will draw heavy loads.
There will be no breaching of walls,
   no going into captivity,
   no cry of distress in our streets.

¹⁵ Blessed are the people of whom this is true;
   blessed are the people whose God is the LORD.

Three Keys to Peace

When W. B. Davidson was a young boy, he walked with his father three miles from his rural home to his grandmother's house. While they were visiting, the sun set. Davidson writes, "Between our home and grandmother's house was a swamp. That night the croaking of the frogs, the chirping of the crickets, and the shadows of the trees frightened me. I asked my father if there was any danger of something catching us, but he assured me that there was nothing to dread.

And so, taking me by the hand, he said, 'I will not allow anything to harm you.' Immediately my fears passed away and I was ready to face the world."

Someone has said that the three keys to real peace are fret not, faint not, fear not.

1. Fret not—because God loves you (1 John 4:16).
2. Faint not—because God holds you (Psalm 139:10).
3. Fear not—because God keeps you (Psalm 121:5).

As we rest in the love of Christ and recognize that God holds our hand, we too shall be at peace and unafraid. The "three keys to real peace"—fret not, faint not, fear not—can open our prison of worry and discouragement. Let's step out into the full joy and liberty of the children of God!

—*Henry Bosch*

Psalm 145:10–21

¹⁰All you have made will praise you, O LORD;
  your saints will extol you.
¹¹They will tell of the glory of your kingdom
  and speak of your might,
¹²so that all men may know of your mighty acts
  and the glorious splendor of your kingdom.
¹³Your kingdom is an everlasting kingdom,
  and your dominion endures through all generations.

The LORD is faithful to all his promises
  and loving toward all he has made.
¹⁴The LORD upholds all those who fall
  and lifts up all who are bowed down.
¹⁵The eyes of all look to you,
  and you give them their food at the proper time.
¹⁶You open your hand
  and satisfy the desires of every living thing.

¹⁷The LORD is righteous in all his ways
  and loving toward all he has made.
¹⁸The LORD is near to all who call on him,
  to all who call on him in truth.
¹⁹He fulfills the desires of those who fear him;
  he hears their cry and saves them.
²⁰The LORD watches over all who love him,
  but all the wicked he will destroy.

²¹My mouth will speak in praise of the LORD.
  Let every creature praise his holy name
  for ever and ever.

Equal Access

Pastor Stuart Silvester told me of a conversation he had with an acquaintance who frequently flew his small private plane in and out of Toronto International Airport. He asked the pilot if he ever encountered problems taking off and landing a small craft at an airport that was dominated by so many large jets. His friend responded, "My plane may be small, but I have the same rights, the same privileges, and the same access to that airport as anyone else—even the jumbo jets!"

Pastor Silvester then made this spiritual application: "It's the same with prayer, with the believer's approach to the throne of grace. No matter who we are or how small we are in comparison with others or how low our station in life, we take a back seat to no one. No one is given priority treatment."

In a world that offers preferential treatment to the wealthy, the famous, and the influential, it's encouraging to know that every child of God has equal access to the Father in heaven. The psalmist said, "The LORD is near to all who call on him, to all who call on him in truth" (Psalm 145:18).

With that assurance, we can "come confidently to the throne of grace" in prayer, knowing that our loving God will never turn us away.

—*Richard DeHaan*

Psalm 146

[1] Praise the LORD!

Praise the LORD, O my soul!
[2] While I live I will praise the LORD;
    I will sing praises to my God while I have my being.

[3] Do not put your trust in princes,
    Nor in a son of man, in whom there is no help.
[4] His spirit departs, he returns to his earth;
    In that very day his plans perish.

[5] Happy is he who has the God of Jacob for his help,
    Whose hope is in the LORD his God,
[6] Who made heaven and earth,
    The sea, and all that is in them;
    Who keeps truth forever,
[7] Who executes justice for the oppressed,
    Who gives food to the hungry.
    The LORD gives freedom to the prisoners.

[8] The LORD opens the eyes of the blind;
    The LORD raises those who are bowed down;
    The LORD loves the righteous.
[9] The LORD watches over the strangers;
    He relieves the fatherless and widow;
    But the way of the wicked He turns upside down.

[10] The LORD shall reign forever—
    Your God, O Zion, to all generations.

Praise the LORD!

(NKJV)

How to Be Happy

Everyone wants to be happy. But many fail in their quest to find that elusive prize because they are looking in the wrong places.

Proverbs 16:20 tells us, "Whoever trusts in the Lord, happy is he." And Psalm 146:5 indicates that happiness comes to those who find their help and hope in God.

The foundation for happiness is a proper relationship with the Lord. But to fully experience that happiness, we must build on that foundation in practical ways. I found this list of Ten Rules for Happier Living:

1. Give something away.
2. Do a kindness.
3. Give thanks always.
4. Work with vim and vigor.
5. Visit the elderly and learn from their experience.
6. Look intently into the face of a baby and marvel.
7. Laugh often—it's life's lubricant.
8. Pray to know God's way.
9. Plan as though you will live forever—you will.
10. Live as though today is your last day on earth.

These are excellent ideas for living a happy life. Undergird each of these rules with praise, and your happiness will be complete. "Praise the Lord, O my soul! While I live I will praise the Lord" (Psalm 146:1–2).

—Richard DeHaan

Psalm 147:1–11

¹Praise the LORD.

How good it is to sing praises to our God,
    how pleasant and fitting to praise him!

²The LORD builds up Jerusalem;
    he gathers the exiles of Israel.
³He heals the brokenhearted
    and binds up their wounds.

⁴He determines the number of the stars
    and calls them each by name.
⁵Great is our Lord and mighty in power;
    his understanding has no limit.
⁶The LORD sustains the humble
    but casts the wicked to the ground.

⁷Sing to the LORD with thanksgiving;
    make music to our God on the harp.
⁸He covers the sky with clouds;
    he supplies the earth with rain
    and makes grass grow on the hills.
⁹He provides food for the cattle
    and for the young ravens when they call.

¹⁰His pleasure is not in the strength of the horse,
    nor his delight in the legs of a man;
¹¹the LORD delights in those who fear him,
    who put their hope in his unfailing love.

A Tender and Mighty God

God knows and numbers the stars, yet He is concerned about you and me, even though we're broken by sin. He binds our shattered hearts with sensitivity and kindness, and He brings healing into the depths of our souls. The greatness of God's power is the greatness of His heart. His strength is the measure of His love. He is a tender and mighty God.

The psalmist tells us that God "determines the number of the stars," and even "calls them each by name" (Psalm 147:4). Would He care for the stars that are mere matter and not care for us, who bear His image? Of course not. He knows about our lonely struggles, and He cares. It is His business to care.

God, in the form of His Son Jesus, was subject to all our passions (Hebrews 2:18). He understands and does not scold or condemn when we fall short and fail. He leans down and listens to our cries for help. He gently corrects us. He heals through time and with great skill.

The stars will fall from the sky someday. They are not God's major concern—you are! He "is able to keep you from falling and to present you before his glorious presence without fault and with great joy" (Jude 1:24). And He will do it!

—*David Roper*

Psalm 149

[1] Praise the LORD.

Sing to the LORD a new song,
 his praise in the assembly of the saints.

[2] Let Israel rejoice in their Maker;
 let the people of Zion be glad in their King.
[3] Let them praise his name with dancing
 and make music to him with tambourine and harp.
[4] For the LORD takes delight in his people;
 he crowns the humble with salvation.
[5] Let the saints rejoice in this honor
 and sing for joy on their beds.

[6] May the praise of God be in their mouths
 and a double-edged sword in their hands,
[7] to inflict vengeance on the nations
 and punishment on the peoples,
[8] to bind their kings with fetters,
 their nobles with shackles of iron,
[9] to carry out the sentence written against them.
 This is the glory of all his saints.

Praise the LORD.

Hymns of Praise

Music is one of those good things in life we take for granted. Yet, as is so often the case, sinful man has taken this good gift from God and used it to serve evil purposes. In our day we're especially aware of its misuse and of the shameful lyrics that so often are a part of it. Good music, however, is a blessing from the Lord. It's a soothing tonic for troubled hearts. It can motivate us to live for Christ, and through it we can lift our hearts in praise to the Lord. Without music, we would be greatly deprived.

An old Jewish legend says that after God had created the world He called the angels to himself and asked them what they thought of it. One of them said, "The only thing lacking is the sound of praise to the Creator." So God created music, and it was heard in the whisper of the wind and in the song of the birds. He also gave man the gift of song. And throughout all the ages, music has blessed multitudes of people.

Singing God's praises honors the Lord, edifies our brothers and sisters in Christ, and brings us joy. As we join with other Christians in singing, it should be with a renewed appreciation of music. So let us join voices with fellow believers and lift our hearts in hymns of praise whenever we have the privilege.

—Richard DeHaan

Psalm 150

[1] Praise the LORD.

Praise God in his sanctuary;
 praise him in his mighty heavens.
[2] Praise him for his acts of power;
 praise him for his surpassing greatness.
[3] Praise him with the sounding of the trumpet,
 praise him with the harp and lyre,
[4] praise him with tambourine and dancing,
 praise him with the strings and flute,
[5] praise him with the clash of cymbals,
 praise him with resounding cymbals.

[6] Let everything that has breath praise the LORD.

Praise the LORD.

A Lesson in Praise

Psalm 150 is not only a beautiful expression of praise, it's also a lesson in praising the Lord. It tells us where to praise, why we're to praise, how we're to praise, and who should offer praise.

Where do we praise? In God's "sanctuary" and "mighty heavens" (v. 1). Wherever we are in the world is a proper place to praise the One who created all things.

Why do we praise? First, because of what God does. He performs "acts of power." Second, because of who God is. The psalmist praised Him for "his surpassing greatness" (v. 2). The all-powerful Creator is the Sustainer of the universe.

How should we praise? Loudly. Softly. Soothingly. Enthusiastically. Rhythmically. Boldly. Unexpectedly. Fearlessly. In other words, we can praise God in many ways and on many occasions (vv. 3–5).

Who should praise? "Everything that has breath" (v. 6). Young and old. Rich and poor. Weak and strong. Every living creature. God's will is for everyone to whom He gave the breath of life to use that breath to acknowledge His power and greatness.

Praise is our enthusiastic expression of gratitude to God for reigning in glory forever.

—Julie Ackerman Link

Index

Note to the Reader

The publisher invites you to share your response to the message of this book by writing Discovery House Publishers, P.O. Box 3566, Grand Rapids, MI 49501, U.S.A. For information about other Discovery House books, music, videos, or DVDs, contact us at the same address or call 1-800-653-8333. Find us on the Internet at http://www.dhp.org/ or send e-mail to books@dhp.org.